ONCE UPON a
RHYME

WARWICKSHIRE &
THE WEST MIDLANDS

Edited by Helen Davies

First published in Great Britain in 2011 by:

 Young**Writers**

Young Writers
Remus House
Coltsfoot Drive
Peterborough
PE2 9BF
Telephone: 01733 890066
Website: www.youngwriters.co.uk

THIS BOOK BELONGS TO

....

Foreword

Here at Young Writers our objective is to help children discover the joys of poetry and creative writing. Few things are more encouraging for the aspiring writer than seeing their own work in print. We are proud that our anthologies are able to give young authors this unique sense of confidence and pride in their abilities.

Once Upon A Rhyme is our latest fantastic competition, specifically designed to encourage the writing skills of primary school children through the medium of poetry. From the high quality of entries received, it is clear that Once Upon A Rhyme really captured the imagination of all involved.

The resulting collection is an excellent showcase for the poetic talents of the younger generation and we are sure you will be charmed and inspired by it, both now and in the future.

Contents

Maddie Stewart is our featured poet this year. She has written a nonsense workshop for you and included some of her great poems. You can find these at the end of your book

Kinlet CE Primary School, Kinlet

Mesty Croft Primary School, Wednesbury

Queen's CE Junior School, Nuneaton

Roberts Primary School, Dudley

St Benedict's Catholic Primary School, Mancetter

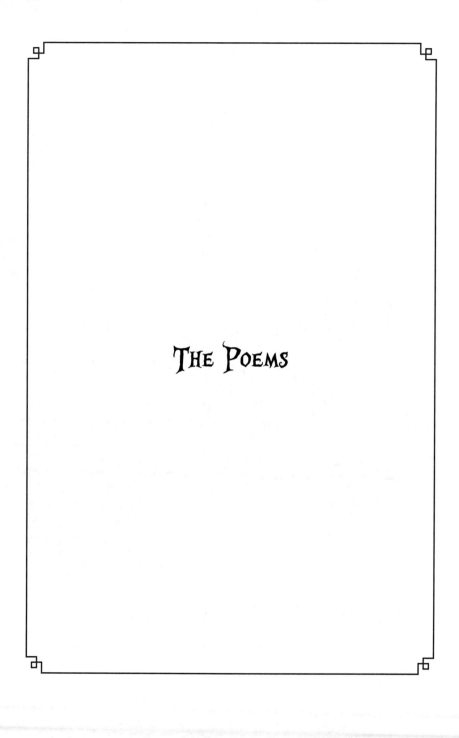

THE POEMS

Chocolate Button

I love my chocolate button,
my button's dear to me,
my chocolate button's nice and dark,
as dark as Mum's strong tea!

I take it out to town,
or maybe just for a walk,
I wish some day, just like me,
my button would start to talk.

Today we're going on holiday,
I'm ready for a fun day.
Of course I'm gonna bring my button,
let's go to the beach and play.

The sun was beating down,
in the warmth I knelt.
But suddenly, to my surprise . . .
my button had begun to melt!

Sophie Scott (11)
All Saints' CE Junior School, Warwick

Where's My Pencil?

'Where's my pencil? Where's my pencil?'
I ask everyone. They all laugh.
Why, because I'm using a spare.

Where's my pencil? Where's my pencil?
I look everywhere
I look in the corner, on the floor, in my pencil case.
Even on my chair.

I go outside (still a pencil short)
and a stick in my hand.
I throw it on the road,
now I understand!

Where's my pencil? Where's my pencil?
In pieces on the road!
Now my questions are answered!

Charlie Widmer (11)
All Saints' CE Junior School, Warwick

Snail

Slithering slowly along the paved path,
Leaving a shiny trail of slime,
Carrying a colourful shell on its back,
Journeys like a silent ghost across the garden.

Savaging the plants with its tiny teeth,
Munching on the prized vegetables,
Dodges the snail repellent,
Slithers on to its secret place.

Chloe Wiltshire (10)
All Saints' CE Junior School, Warwick

School

All you do in school
is work - listen - fun.
When you're in the playground,
it's run, run, run!

When it's the end of break,
we have a sigh.
When it's home time,
it's time to say goodbye.

Francesca Salter (9)
All Saints' CE Junior School, Warwick

Who Started It?

Hitler started it,
Hitler started it,
and Churchill ended it.

We invaded Germany and saved the Jews,
well some of them.

Russians invaded Berlin and found Hitler dead.
Good always wins.

Kurt Allright (11)
All Saints' CE Junior School, Warwick

Bob Vs Blob Rap

A long time ago, in a place far away,
An alien crashed and landed in farmer Bob's hay,
The hay launched up and landed with a smash,
The alien went through the floor and screamed, 'Where's my cash?'
Bob lay down and the cattle heard a crash,
The alien jumped through the house and landed with a bash.

The alien crept out of sight,
Farmer Bob looked for him to have a fight.
Suddenly he grasped a knife,
Bob looked for him all through the dead of night.
Until the alien hurt Bob,
Bob saw a humongous Blob until . . .

The Blob shaped into a tree,
I hope he doesn't do that to me!
They both had guns, they shot from a hill,
Bob was ready to have a kill!

To be continued . . .

Max Mallen-Freeman (9)
Astley CE Primary School, Stourport-on-Severn

A Dragon Rap

A long time ago, in a place far away,
Suddenly I found a dragon being slain.
I scrambled to help the struggling knight,
I got my armour and started to fight.
All the neighbours were shivering in fear,
I stabbed the dragon with my deathly spear.

The dragon bellowed with a mighty rage,
The knight put him in a soundless cage.
He hooked him up on a very big Jeep,
The knight drove off and shouted, 'See ya creep!'

Thomas Ablett (9)
Astley CE Primary School, Stourport-on-Severn

Titanic Rap

A long time ago in a place far away,
A gigantic ship set sail on her way.
People were singing and dancing on the deck,
Totally unaware that the ship would be a wreck.
Invisible icebergs slammed into her side,
An enormous gash had opened her up wide.

In the dead of night, people were shrieking,
Families gathering as the ship was creaking,
Water crashing through her glass dome,
Gruesome bodies floating in the foam,
The *boom* of a shot rang into the air,
A desperate call for help just was not there.

The captain quite alone, his bridge all dim,
A silent chill gathering all around him,
Her giant stern rose high into the sky,
Breaking her back before she had to die.

Henry Dover-Porter (9)
Astley CE Primary School, Stourport-on-Severn

The Monster Rap

A long time ago, in a place far away,
There lived a monster who loved to play.
His teeth were yellow, his nose was red,
The only thing he ate was wholemeal bread.
One dark night he had a great fright,
He woke up and saw the lightning strike.

He spied out the window and saw that thing,
He really was wearing a lot of bling.
The weighty punk turned around,
Then stomped over the muddy ground.
Suddenly the monster threw a punch,
Then decided to eat his lunch.

Now the monster ate his lunch,
He still wanted something to munch.
He went into town, searching for more,
Then he let out a mighty roar . . .

Harry Williams (10)
Astley CE Primary School, Stourport-on-Severn

Kindness Rap

A long time ago in a place far away,
Where princesses danced in the month of May.
Where brave knights fought and maidens sang,
Where monsters exploded with a deafening bang,
A dragon called Jerry, big and mean,
Learns to be kind in this next scene.

Sulky Jerry out for a stroll,
Came up against an ugly troll.
She gave a bow and a sorry smile,
And also gave a big red tile.
Carved on the stone was his mother's will,
And within a frightful bill.

Poor old Jerry weeping with distress,
Picturing his mother in a beautiful dress.
For all life has dismayed sadness,
But through a tear out trickles badness!

Catherine Coulthard (9)
Astley CE Primary School, Stourport-on-Severn

Monster Rap

A long time ago in a place far away,
An old monster came out to play.
He sneaked out of his maze,
Wandering around in a daze.
He slumped right down to do a puzzle,
Whilst wearing his giant muzzle.

His favourite game was chess,
But he always looked a mess.
He liked to eat hunks of meat,
As his special treat.
He was a very big beast, he always liked a feast,
He made bread with tall rising yeast.

He climbed the tall, rotten mound,
Leaping up with a great big bound.
But this big beast, who was he?
We don't know, it was a mystery . . .

Oliver Daniels (11)
Astley CE Primary School, Stourport-on-Severn

Monster Rap

A long time ago in a place far away,
A monster munched on a piece of hay,
He felt lonely, he wanted a friend,
Then, he stomped to peek round the bend,
There was no one there, he put on a frown,
Then he decided to look round town.

Searching for a friend wasn't very fun,
He got hot and sweaty from looking at the sun,
He climbed a tree to have a rest,
When he woke the sight was the best,
The friend he had been looking for was there,
Even though it looked like a bear!

As soon as he saw her they wanted to play,
The beautiful bear's name was Faye,
A butterfly was flying which Faye caught,
But was Faye as lovely as he thought . . . ?

Caitlin Bean (10)
Astley CE Primary School, Stourport-on-Severn

The Monster Rap

A long time ago in a place far away,
Lived a great big monster, who slept in a tray.
He was totally grey and had thirty-nine eyes,
He had ten arms and plump giant thighs.
For his food he ate the houses of a town,
The people of the town said he was going down.

The people of the town would blow up the creature,
Before he tried to make another horror feature.
They put some TNT under the monster's lair,
They set up a trap which was sure to ensnare.
The plunger was up and the dynamite ready,
It was a synch, it was sure to stay steady.

The monster went back to his comfy tray,
But then he saw where the dynamite lay.
The creature knew he had come to his doom,
And he went up with an enormous *boom!*

Hugh Badger (10)
Astley CE Primary School, Stourport-on-Severn

The Mysterious Rap

A long time ago, in a place far away,
A princess danced in the month of May,
Her favourite hobby was reading a book,
Followed by being able to cook,
She was in danger, I don't know why,
Maybe someone was lurking nearby.

'A bear!' the guards shrieked as they ran with fright,
In the twirling mist, appeared a shiny knight,
Who came to save the princess so fair,
But then he saw the fierce, grizzly bear . . .

Tarnia Jordan (10)
Astley CE Primary School, Stourport-on-Severn

Piglet Rap

A long time ago, in a place far away,
Two little piglets in a house of hay.
One was pink, one was red,
The red one always stayed in bed.
The red one was lazy and the pink one was smart,
And it had a healthy heart.

The pink one always wins,
And sometimes sings hymns.
The red one has his own mind,
And learns to be kind!

Elleshia Bower (9)
Astley CE Primary School, Stourport-on-Severn

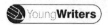

Monster Rap

A long time ago, in a place far away,
A monster decided he wanted to play.
He rose up growling from the rotten ground,
To climb up the steep, muddy mound.
He stood like a tower, he was that tall,
Everyone he saw he thought was small.

The very next day, he went to town,
Then he realised, it was a long way down.
An extremely old man, limped right past,
So the monster chose to gobble him fast!

Richie Parker (11)
Astley CE Primary School, Stourport-on-Severn

Gore Rap

A long time ago, in a place far away,
A huge war raged through the month of May.
Stinking, blood, guts and gore,
Trickled all over the rotten floor.
The dead spread on the treacherous field,
As they travelled to the dead unhealed.

They advanced to Heaven in armies still,
But then they sighted their very next kill.
Jaws wide open, teeth like knives,
These new foes were mutant pies!

Sam Branford (11)
Astley CE Primary School, Stourport-on-Severn

A Slimy Rap

A long time ago, in a place far away,
The slimy slug, wanted to play.
But he was so slimy, no one liked him,
Not even Jim the snail, nor did Tim.
Jim and Tim were identical twins,
Who kept poking each other with pins.

The slug called Slime who couldn't tell the time,
Was struggling with a mountain he had to climb.
He loved to race all over the place.

Patrick Nightingale (10)
Astley CE Primary School, Stourport-on-Severn

History

I love history,
It's all I ever do.
Have you heard about the Tudors?
If you haven't they'll torture you.

Henry VIII might be looking for a wife.
If you say no he'll be mad.
He might even stab you with a knife,
Or the Tudor way - hung, drawn and quartered.

You don't want to hear about the Vikings,
All they did was fight.
Stick with Freya, the goddess of love,
No Viking will get you in May,
Because guess what, that's their fighting day.

Do you want to be a Victorian?
I should say not.
Victoria makes you work all day,
For schools, your pay is not a lot.

So let me go through it again,
Terrible Tudors torture,
Vulnerable Vikings fight,
Vile Victorian children work
All through the night.

Caitlin Leigh Bird (9)
Barlestone CE Primary School, Barlestone

Celebrities

All these celebrities - different types,
getting awards under the spotlights.
Piers Morgan laughing out his jokes,
Cheryl Cole talking sweet to the folks.

Tinie Tempah rapping as he talks,
Sharon Osbourne hiding all her warts.
Gilly McKeith watching what we eat,
Jamie Oliver cooking all the meat.

Justin Bieber sorting out his hair,
All the others getting presented by the mayor.
Singing Beyoncé with her big, big hips,
Dolly Parton with her blown-up lips.

Cee Lo Green singing Forget You,
Simon Cowell saying 'moo-moo!'
Dannii Minogue always on the phone,
then Rhianna checking out her skin tone.

Katie Price breaking up every minute,
Usher telling everyone to hit it.
Ant and Dec on 'Get Me Out Of Here',
Miley Cyrus so happy, she's got a tear.

Ozzy Osbourne with his round glasses,
Amanda Holden putting on her false lashes.
Kim bossing people to clean their houses,
Aggro Santos dancing his dances.

All these celebrities from all over the world,
which celeb do you fancy? Tell me, *word*!

Sasha Belcher (9)
Barlestone CE Primary School, Barlestone

Little Bo

Once upon a rhyme,
In a very weird time
There was a time where all the nursery rhymes were alive
And at parties they did the jive.
There was one rhyme that wouldn't behave
Who was always exploring caves.

Can you guess who it is?
Who has a personality with a fizz!
Do you have a clue
Who else this person might be?
Well wouldn't you like to know!
I'll put you out of your misery, it's 'Little Bo'.

Little Bo Peep
Was always losing her sheep.
Causing havoc
Especially in the horses' paddock.

Little Bo Peep
Once lost her sheep
But little did she know, that her sheep had followed her to school.
When she got there all of the kids started to be cruel.
Little Bo Peep started to feel sad
And that was when she turned bad.

Now Bo Peep misbehaves
And ties people up in caves.
So just remember next time you visit Poetry Land
Watch out for Little Bo down near the sand.

Grace Kearns (9)
Barlestone CE Primary School, Barlestone

American Football

In American football you need to run fast,
And you need a kit or you'll get bashed.
If you want to score you need a touchdown,
Then the other team will have a frown.

An American football is shaped like a brown rugby ball
Be careful because you might get tackled and fall.
Some of the American football players are mean,
But some of the players are keen.

In American football there are Y-shaped poles
And sometimes moles dig their holes.
It usually takes place on a field,
And some of the players use their arms as shields.

In American football, you get changed in a changing room
And sometimes when you play you face your doom.
An American football player wears head gear,
And after a match they always go for a beer.

American football is really rough
And if you want to make it you've got to be tough.
Most of the players are very strong.
And the worst armour you can wear is a thong.

Ethan Crumbie (9)
Barlestone CE Primary School, Barlestone

I Am A Zombie

I am a zombie and I kill people,
My eyes light up.
I have a pet zombie dog called Frank
People are scared of me.
I am vicious.
I am a zombie - I walk and I'm dumb.
I have lots of friends; Danny, Barry, Harry and Jammy.
We break into buildings.
I'll tell you something - it's cool.
We live everywhere and go everywhere.
Me and my friends keep together.
My life is awesome.

Jamie Disley (9)
Barlestone CE Primary School, Barlestone

The Barbecue

I go out to play
After school today.
My mum is setting up the barbecue
Just for us two.

We have onions that make you cry,
And we have tasty burgers that you want to buy.

My mum is really good at doing a barbecue,
But now it's not just for us two.
Now the barbecue is for everyone,
And some people buy more than one.

The barbecue is open nearly every day,
And the hot dogs are not much to pay.
After a long busy day,
I can't wait till another day.

Now it is night-time,
It's time to end my rhyme.

Ellen Chiswell (9)
Barlestone CE Primary School, Barlestone

Zombies

Z ooming zombies attack people,
O ff go the lights.
M ega strong zombies,
B ig zombie dogs on fire.
I s that a cruel zombie?
E mily's my name.
S cary zombies are my game.

Z ombies looking at me,
O MG, they're eating me.
M illy is eating me,
B eat them down now.
I hate zombies,
E xcept Erin.
S he bites but not a lot.

Emily Statham (9)
Barlestone CE Primary School, Barlestone

Aliens In The Castle

One day with all the king's horses and all the king's men
It was a very nice day for the king but then . . .
A huge spacecraft came out of the sky!
A little group of little aliens came out but why?

They came from the planet Mars
The people ran on horses and in cars.
The aliens were very sad
They had not been bad . . .

They saw the castle, it was big and wide
The king had seen and let them inside
They were very, very good mates
The aliens loved the castle, it had really good gates
But most of all the castle was really tall.
The aliens had their lunch, they though it was cool.

The aliens went back in their UFO, but why?
The aliens had to say goodbye, but it made the king cry.

Aidan Gallagher (9)
Barlestone CE Primary School, Barlestone

Running In A Race

I'm second in a race,
I've got a pale face.
I think I'm going to come first,
But I think I'm going to burst.

I think I'm getting wet,
I think it's from the sweat.
I want to stop but,
I can't because it's hot.

The amazing acrobat doing a flip,
I can't stop because I'm doing a skip.
I'm going past the first one! But . . .
It's the finish, I've won, yes!

Abbie Blackery (8)
Barlestone CE Primary School, Barlestone

Football

Football, it's such fun,
when they play under the sun.
On the pitch where goals are scored,
and goalkeepers get bored.

All the teams are so competitive,
and the players are so repetitive.
When it starts to rain,
everyone thinks it's a pain.

Leicester City are so good,
but when it rains they wear a hood.
Sometimes when they're training,
it always starts raining.

Lewis Underwood (10)
Barlestone CE Primary School, Barlestone

Dogs

Dogs hate it if you blow in their faces,
It will make them nasty.
There are lots of different breeds of dogs.
Dogs love to go on walks.
Most dogs are really friendly and love to play.
Dogs can sometimes be really funny,
When they chase their tails.
Most dogs I know, if you brush their necks, they smile.
Dogs roll on their backs if they have an itch
Or if they want their bellies tickling.
Dogs always greet people who they see.
Dogs are really sweet and nice.

Jaidan Underwood (9)
Barlestone CE Primary School, Barlestone

Space

Space is dark and gloomy too,
It's spinning like the moon.
So come with me and you'll see,
The sun shine like the moon.

Space has all different planets,
Like Jupiter and Mars and more.
So look at the solar system,
It's as big as the big bang.

The universe is like a dot,
The stars are like a twinkle.

Courtney Green (10)
Barlestone CE Primary School, Barlestone

My Favourite Pet Is A Dog

My favourite pet is a dog,
He rolls around in the bog.
He likes his new name,
Although he's quite plain.
As long as I love him so,
Sometimes he hugs my toe.

I took him for a walk one day,
And took him for a good play.
I went to the café and put him in a dog zone,
But I'd only just realised that I'd forgotten to give him a bone!

Erin Bebb (10)
Barlestone CE Primary School, Barlestone

Love

Love is in the air
Spinning like a red pear
I love my romantic hair
It looks like a bear
I love Nell.

Nell has long hair
It floats in the air
She is so small
She is good at football.
I love Nell.

Ciaran Irvine (10)
Barlestone CE Primary School, Barlestone

Science

E xcellent
R ough
U nhealthy
P ossible
T empting
I mpressive
O riginal
N oticeable
S mooth.

Connor Wycherley (10)
Barlestone CE Primary School, Barlestone

Art

All drawings are made up in my head,
I even draw after I've gone to bed.
I can draw the moon,
Or even a baboon.

Art is really cool,
All you have to do is follow the rules.
This is the end of my art rap,
Now it's time to take a nap.

Billy Noon (9)
Barlestone CE Primary School, Barlestone

Space

When I grow up I am going into space,
I think it is cool and very ace.
I really want to go in a ship,
And while I'm in it I will do a flip.

Space is scary, the stars shine brightly,
The stars stick together tightly.
I'll meet an alien called Bob . . .

George Walters (9)
Barlestone CE Primary School, Barlestone

Wally The Whale

Gentle monster of the sea
Swimming in the dark blue ocean.
Whales are like people,
They have their own feelings.
Leave them alone
Let them be free.

As the whaling ships move in.
Gentle creatures huddle in.
Boom! Boom! Boom!
The guns are near.
Scared and frightened screams
We all hear.

Whaling is cruel.
Stop it right now!
Listen to me
And leave them alone!
Gentle monster of the sea
I really do care, as you can see.

Hannah Shakeshaft (8)
Cockshutt CE Primary School, Cockshutt

Tiger, Tiger

Tiger, tiger
Wild and free
Chasing meat round and round.
Then *boom!*
Shot to the ground,
Trapped in a cage,
Eyes so scared
Skin removed
Eyes and bones made into cures.

Elephant, elephant
Gentle and kind
Splashing in a pool
In a game reserve,
They're so happy.
Then *bang!*
Dead in one.
Tusks removed,
So prized.

Poppy Rosser (10)
Cockshutt CE Primary School, Cockshutt

The Whales

Whales, whales in the sea
Whales, whales for you and me
Watch their backs rise and fall,
As they move then seem to haul their bodies out
Of the water.
Their gaping mouths eat all the krill
Then filter the water through their gills
These gentle giants in the water.
People harpoon them to get their meat
It isn't fair you know, they are part of the world as well.
They let out a shrill scream to call for help
But it is too late
The whales will soon be no more because of the human race.
Stop harpooning them - they deserve to live,
These graceful mammals should be here on this planet,
Here on this planet today and forever.

Claire Sankey (9)
Cockshutt CE Primary School, Cockshutt

The Fox

Who is this wonderful creature
who walks on four feet?
Why is this creature so quick and kills his
prey in one bite?
Orange, red, black, grey and white.

Why do we want to kill him, this beautiful creature?
He sleeps, breeds and feeds.
So why do we want to kill him?
Most hate him and want to kill him.
Why?

Why do we want to harm him when he lives
like we do?
Why is this wonderful creature harmed with
our human ways?

Rhiannon Jones (10)
Cockshutt CE Primary School, Cockshutt

Global Warming

Global warming is one big problem.
If we don't stop,
There's going to be extinction.
Every tree that is chopped down,
Is hurting the Earth so much.
We need to stop
Or where are we going to live?
The ice is melting as we speak,
Animals are losing their numbers week by week,
The forest is being chopped down, thousands a day.
The Earth is one big disgrace!

Pippa Bowers (9)
Cockshutt CE Primary School, Cockshutt

The Brown Wonder

The bush baby is a brown wonder,
Sleek in the trees
It cries when it's scared.
Nocturnal, it sleeps in the day.
The bush baby clings to a tree like a log.
The bush baby is a brown wonder.

Why kill them?
Why set fires?
We need to protect them from you.
So next time think.

Thorin Dhillon-Peters (9)
Cockshutt CE Primary School, Cockshutt

Homeless People

One day a person was stranded
On the pavement
Who had a sign saying:
Homeless and hungry
He had to sleep in the rainy outside world.

The next day he didn't have
Any food or water
No one to cuddle up to
Whenever he was cold.

William Mackrell (10)
Cockshutt CE Primary School, Cockshutt

Me And My Life

Lord please help this baby being born,
care and love so you can give me a home.
So then we can sit down and settle in.
Then we can snuggle down on the rug
and give me a hug.

It is really hard for me,
I have nothing left in my life.
Please give me a new life to get better.

Leah Birch (11)
Cockshutt CE Primary School, Cockshutt

Afghanistan

The war is terrible.
It has begun in
Afghanistan.
As bombs go bang
And children moan.

Troops hide in bunkers
With their firing guns.
People are dying in
Hospital or alone.

Edward Shakeshaft (10)
Cockshutt CE Primary School, Cockshutt

Children With Disabilities

Please help the children in wheelchairs
That had accidents like car crashes
And falling off bikes
It can
Be very dangerous
She is a nice girl
She would like to walk
But she is in a wheelchair.

Bradley Barnett (9)
Cockshutt CE Primary School, Cockshutt

Polar Bears

Please help polar bears
Two polar bears are
Stuck on a piece of ice
It is melting.
The thin ice will break
They are good swimmers
What about the baby?
Will it go under?

Molly Twigg (8)
Cockshutt CE Primary School, Cockshutt

Species

There are only certain species around the world
Please help and keep the animals safe
Don't collect elephant tusks
There are only 300 gorillas around the world.

Tom Twigg (8)
Cockshutt CE Primary School, Cockshutt

My Dancing Diamond

My dancing diamond loves to dance,
He went to a party and lost his pants.
After he came to me and said, 'My pants are lost.'
I was so cross, but someone came and said it was Mr Frost.
I bought him new pants and he was really happy,
He went home a happy chappy.
He was really happy, I decided to give him a new top,
Then accidentally I hit him with a mop.
He screamed, shouted and cried,
'That was on purpose,' he sighed.
My dancing diamond is called Sid,
I bought him from the auction at a high bid,
He is truly my bestest friend,
Without him my life would end.

Nabila Ahmed (9)
Hateley Heath Primary School, Hateley Heath

Our Best Friend Kaylee

Our best friend Kaylee is really funny
And she likes to eat honey.
She likes to jump on the tyres
But it also makes her really tired.
She has green eyes
And she loves to hide.
She is a girl
And she likes to twirl.
She is eight
And we are her best mates.

Zuzana Moscakova & Jayden Hackett (7)
Hateley Heath Primary School, Hateley Heath

Food

Food, beautiful food,
Sausage, egg and bacon.
Food, beautiful food
Puts me in a hungry mood.

The thought of food makes me smile.
I can smell it from a mile.
Broccoli is so vile.
Big and green like a crocodile.

Food, beautiful food.
Rice, chicken and stewed.
Food, beautiful food
Puts me in a hungry mood.

Paramveer Singh (9)
Hateley Heath Primary School, Hateley Heath

The Life Of A Diamond

Diamonds are pretty,
They are so nice,
They are always so very bright,
But they never bite.

Diamonds are bright,
Like a shining light,
They jump up and down,
All day and night.

Diamonds are rare,
They always sit and glare,
All day they sit and stare.

Gemma Louise Fox (9)
Hateley Heath Primary School, Hateley Heath

Sparkly Diamond

Diamond, diamond, you're so beautiful.
You make the light shiny in the night.
You will not get scratched by cats.
Diamond, diamond, you're so cool.
You make the people love you.

Diamond, diamond comes to town.
Want to make you into a crown.
Diamond, diamond, you make my eyes
Sparkle like the stars in the sky.
Diamond, diamond, you're so nice.
You really look like the night lights.

Muhammed Ndow (8)
Hateley Heath Primary School, Hateley Heath

Sparkly Diamonds

Diamonds are the best
Da dom dad a dom
They can never be scratched
Da dom dad a dom
Diamonds are the best
Da dom dad a dom
They are very rare
Da dom dad a dom
Diamonds are so special
Da dom dad a dom
They mean forever.

Vinay Chandel (8)
Hateley Heath Primary School, Hateley Heath

The Princess

The princess wore a pink, beautiful star dress.
When the clock struck twelve her dress was a mess.
She ran and ran all the way home.
Then she was crying all alone.
The prince came with her shoe and said, 'Will this fit you?
Because dear Cinders, I love you.'

Ria Gharu (7) & Amanpreet Shergill (8)
Hateley Heath Primary School, Hateley Heath

Diamond

Diamonds, diamonds are so pretty.
They're even better than a kitty.

Diamonds, diamonds are the best.
Even better than a treasure chest.

They are very bright and light.
Shining away in the night light.

They can be very colourful.
They are rare and meaningful.

Bradley Greenaway (9)
Hateley Heath Primary School, Hateley Heath

Diamonds!

Diamonds, diamonds, as bright as a shining star.
Diamonds, diamonds would fit in a fairy car.
Diamonds come from India.
They belong to a girl called Hindia.
A girl was wearing a diamond boot.
A boy was wearing a diamond suit.
Please, please, please diamond don't break.
Oh for goodness' sake.
Diamonds, diamonds, they're so rare
That last night I saw a diamond bear . . .

Alicia Johnson (8)
Hateley Heath Primary School, Hateley Heath

Indian Cricket Player

He is the best at cricket,
He can score lots of wickets.
He is fit because he eats carrots,
And he has a pet parrot.
In India he lives,
A fright to bowlers he gives.
He gets a massive six,
And bats are broken to bits.
He is Sachin Tendulkar.

Elliot Levi Kailla & Aman Chopra (8)
Hateley Heath Primary School, Hateley Heath

Dashing Diamond

Diamonds are fast.
They will forever last.

My diamond is funny.
Small and cute like a bunny.

Shining like a shooting star.
It is my superstar.

My diamond makes me happy.
Losing it will make me unhappy.

Sana Bi Malik (8)
Hateley Heath Primary School, Hateley Heath

My Best Friend

My best friend is caring
And she likes sharing.

My best friend is always kind.
She's the best friend you can ever find.

My best friend is funny.
She is sweet as honey.

My best friend is really cool.
We talk a lot around school.

Althea Daley & Chelsea Cartwright (9)
Hateley Heath Primary School, Hateley Heath

The Really Fast Pick-Up Truck

George the fast pick-up truck,
Always has lots of luck.

He picks up smashed cars,
And drives them to the planet Mars.

George is two-tonne green,
He has a motorbike friend called Dean.

Dean sounds quite mean,
But he's the nicest bike George has ever seen.

Shaun Jones (8)
Hateley Heath Primary School, Hateley Heath

Diamonds Are Forever

Dishing, dashing diamonds,
On and off my hands,
Fishing, flashing diamonds,
Supposedly they evolved from the sands.

Dishing, dashing diamonds,
Are so bright and pretty
Fishing, flashing diamonds,
You buy them from the city.

Eivina Rokaite (8)
Hateley Heath Primary School, Hateley Heath

Michel

Michel is my best mate.
He is seven but coming eight!
Michel loves to always smile.
He is in my good friend file.

Michel has short hair.
His hair gets me tempted to stare.
Michel's favourite colour is green.
It's the greatest colour he's ever seen.

Michal Horvat & Amice Holden (7)
Hateley Heath Primary School, Hateley Heath

My Best Friend

She is very kind.
She has a wonderful mind.

We always play together.
We will be best friends forever.

She sits with me in class.
I really hope our friendship lasts.

Best friends forever!

Shenille Baker (9)
Hateley Heath Primary School, Hateley Heath

My Forever Bright Diamonds

D iamonds shine
I n the light
A fter dark
M ost diamonds switch
O ff
N ow my
D iamonds
S hine bright all day long.

Jusleen Dulay (8)
Hateley Heath Primary School, Hateley Heath

The Dog On The Roller Coaster

The dog on the roller coaster
reminds me of my favourite poster.
King-Da-Ka, is very fast
as it goes whizzing past.
128 miles per hour,
it uses a lot of power.
The dog Stella slaps herself and wakes.
For goodness' sake.

Alicia Abraham (7) & Hayden Boora (8)
Hateley Heath Primary School, Hateley Heath

Diamond Poem

D iamonds are as precious as can be.
I love diamonds because they are so beautiful.
A diamond is so precious on its own.
M y class found a beautiful diamond.
O ne diamond is worth £10,000, *wow!*
N o one can say that diamonds are not shiny.
D iamonds are precious.
S ome are crystal clear.

Leya Kaylan Smith (8)
Hateley Heath Primary School, Hateley Heath

The Princess

She has golden, glossy hair and she is very fair,
She is really kind to me,
And always makes me a cup of tea.
She saw me and made me a cup of tea.
Her name is Amanpreet.
She is my friend
But I wonder what she says . . .

Rachel Lee (7) & Amanpreet Kaur (8)
Hateley Heath Primary School, Hateley Heath

Diamonds

D iamonds are shiny
I like diamonds because they are the best
A diamond is so precious
M y diamond is called Crystal
O h no, my diamond is a pistol
N obody has got a better diamond than me
D iamonds are the best thing in the world.

Brandon Howells (9)
Hateley Heath Primary School, Hateley Heath

Diamonds Are Beautiful

Diamonds, diamonds are so good
Diamonds, diamonds are gorgeous
Diamonds, diamonds are beautiful
Diamonds, diamonds are shiny
Diamonds, diamonds are lovely
Diamonds, diamonds are cool
Diamonds, diamonds are pretty.

Carlton Timmins (9)
Hateley Heath Primary School, Hateley Heath

Diamonds

Did you know that diamonds are very rare?
In the sky that's where they shine.
A little diamond shines so high, like a star in the sky.
My diamond is very shiny in my living room.
On Tuesday it was green.
Not so long ago it was blue.
Diamonds are very special.

Harry Chander (9)
Hateley Heath Primary School, Hateley Heath

Diamond

D iamond, diamond, dashing diamond.
I ncredible, impressive, interesting diamond.
A mazing, attractive, admiring diamond.
M assive, marvellous, mysterious diamond.
O nly, official, ordinary diamond.
N o one notices, nightly diamond.
D iamond, diamond, dashing diamond.

Fahiza Ahmed (9)
Hateley Heath Primary School, Hateley Heath

The Ninja Baby

The baby likes to kick very hard,
He feels like a lump of lard.

When he is born I would like a hold,
I hope he is as good as gold.

I think we should call him Max,
But watch out because he attacks.

Alexandra Howard (7) & Callan Marriot (8)
Hateley Heath Primary School, Hateley Heath

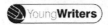

My Best Friend

She is the best girl I know.
Sometimes she has a hairband shaped as a bow.

Sometimes I go to visit her house,
There she shows me her pet mouse.

I love my best friend as she is so kind,
A good friend is so hard to find.

Baljit Kaur (8)
Hateley Heath Primary School, Hateley Heath

Ninja Baby

The ninja baby is round and fat!
Sometimes he's like a tennis bat!

The ninja baby was born in 2002
Also he likes the colour blue!

He once did some naughty fighting,
'Cause he did a bit of biting.

Maria Irfan & Courtney Garbett (7)
Hateley Heath Primary School, Hateley Heath

The Rabbit

The rabbit is as white as snow.
He jumps about really slow.
His ears are big so they can hear
Danger when it is really near.

His belly is as round as a ball.
He bounces all day long.

Leon Harding (7) & Joshua Cartwitght (8)
Hateley Heath Primary School, Hateley Heath

The Princess

The princess had a yellow crown.
Oh my gosh it had gone brown!
The princess had a dress that was pink.
It was made with a spell from ink.
She changed into her pyjamas that were red.
Then at ten o'clock she went off to her bed.

Sabina Dolinska & Nimrah Shabir (7)
Hateley Heath Primary School, Hateley Heath

Wrestlers

Wrestlers, wrestlers, big and strong.
Sometimes wrestlers get it wrong.
Wrestlers, wrestlers slam their opponent on the floor,
Then they go back for some more.
Sometimes wrestlers head for glory.
Hope it's not the end of the story.

Kyle Timmins (7) & Gagandeep Singh (8)
Hateley Heath Primary School, Hateley Heath

Football Teams

Eleven men, strong and true.
Wearing their colours white and blue.
Kicking a ball as they run around.
In front of their fans in a football ground.
Scoring a goal is their only aim
And winning this important game.

Nathan Oyemade (7) & Callam Henry (8)
Hateley Heath Primary School, Hateley Heath

Diamond Poem

Diamonds, diamonds, dashing like shooting stars.
Diamonds, diamonds, shiny, flashing like the sun.
Diamonds are the best all the time.
Diamonds are nice on all sides.
Diamonds are nice all around.

Lucas Peterkin (9)
Hateley Heath Primary School, Hateley Heath

Diamond Poem

Diamonds, diamonds, like shooting stars,
Diamonds, diamonds come from Mars.
Diamonds, diamonds are so pretty,
Diamonds, diamonds are better than a kitty.
Diamonds, diamonds are so great,
People even use them as bait.

Harshdeep Dhillon (9)
Hateley Heath Primary School, Hateley Heath

Diamond Poem

Diamonds, diamonds dazzling like a star
Diamonds, diamonds shine better than a car
Diamonds are shiny, that's a tip
Diamonds cannot be ripped
Diamonds, diamonds do not make people sad
Diamonds, diamonds do not make people mad.

Harry Britton (9)
Hateley Heath Primary School, Hateley Heath

Diamonds

Diamonds are very rare.
Diamonds are shiny.
Diamonds are expensive.
Diamonds are special.
Diamonds are beautiful.
Diamonds are wicked.

Nicholas Marks (8)
Hateley Heath Primary School, Hateley Heath

Fabulous Diamonds

Fabulous diamonds you are so gorgeous,
You make my eyes sparkle like glitter.
In the light you shine and shimmer,
You sparkle and make a rainbow glimmer.

Lauren Marshall (8)
Hateley Heath Primary School, Hateley Heath

The Dinosaur

The T-rex has a tongue like bright red blood,
When he cries he causes a flood.
He has gigantic crinkles on his back,
They get wrinkly when he baths.
He has bright, bright eyes like the sun,
And all his friends think he is fun.

Ethan Phillips, Jack Weston & Rajveer (7)
Hateley Heath Primary School, Hateley Heath

The Ugly Princess

Once there lived an ugly princess named Grace
She smelt so much, she was a big disgrace!
She was so brave but then she was afraid!
She even scared away the maid!
She never even had a friend!
She will come to a sticky end!

Kyra Holden & Brooke Summers (7)
Hateley Heath Primary School, Hateley Heath

Best Friends Forever

Best friends, best friends, always together.
We're always together, forever and ever.
My best friend is really cool.
We talk together a lot at school.
We always play together and we share,
Best friends, best friends, always care.

Selina Malhi (8) & Mariam Joof (9)
Hateley Heath Primary School, Hateley Heath

The Rhino

The rhino is running really fast,
He's in a race and he comes up last.
He gives up and he stamps his feet,
Because he is hungry so he grabs some meat.

Ria Mall & Sinead Lawrence (8)
Hateley Heath Primary School, Hateley Heath

Wolverhampton Wanderers!

W olves are the best
O n target,
L iverpool lose to us,
V olley masters,
E very player is great
R oaring of the fans,
H ennessy with all his saves
A s the Wolves score through Kevin Doyle.
M atty Jarvis with all his pace,
P assing the ball as smoothly as a snake,
T ackles get stuck in.
O 'Hara is the newcomer.
N ever give up.

W est Brom miss the penalty,
A tmosphere,
N oisy fans,
D oyle scores a cracker.
E arache when I get back from the match,
R eally good striker.
E Banks-Blake with all his strength,
R unning to the goal,
S teven Fletcher with all his skill!

Harrison Clowsley (10)
Hinstock Primary School, Hinstock

Amazing Alliteration!

Ten tipsy tarantulas tumbling tremendously!
Slow staring sloths slipping sideways!
Large lazy ladies laughing loudly!
Happy hearty hares hopping home!
Angry aimless apes ambling away!
Wonky wiggly worms wobbling wildly west!
Filthy frightened foxes frantically fleeing from farmers!
Rude racing rascals running round and round!
Perfect preening princesses pedalling proudly past
Boring busy bees buzzing bravely back!

Verity Rogers (10)
Hinstock Primary School, Hinstock

No Word Of A Lie

(Inspired by 'No Word of a Lie' by Jackie Kay)

I've jumped off the tallest school
And that's *no word of a lie!*

I've made the world's largest rubber band ball
And that's *no word of a lie!*

I've been to Mars, Jupiter and space
And that's *no word of a lie!*

I've been wrapped up in shoelaces for one whole weekend
And that's *no word of a lie!*

I can multiply 57,692 by 99,758 in two seconds or less
And that's *no word of a lie!*

I have my own dragon and I made its own lair
And that's *no word of a lie!*

Fine you don't have to believe me do you?
OK, OK, OK
I am the biggest liar in the world
And that's *no word of a lie!*

Eleanor Hainsworth (9)
Hinstock Primary School, Hinstock

No Word Of A Lie!

(Inspired by 'No Word of a Lie!' by Jackie Kay)

I am the best skipper in the school
And that's no word of a lie!

I am the prettiest girl at the ball
And that's no word of a lie!

I am the best inventor at making toys
And that's no word of a lie!

I am the best mentor in the school
And that's no word of a lie!

I can eat 1,000 beefburgers in two seconds
And that's no world of a lie!

Francesca Wakefield (9)
Hinstock Primary School, Hinstock

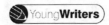

Football Crazy

Football crazy, the whistle blows,
Scoring goals wherever we go.
We play in a claret and blue strip,
Have you guessed what team yet?
Red, yellow cards can be given,
But we don't want any of them,
We need to score as many goals
To keep us at the top.

We play up and down the pitch,
Running fast, we get a stitch.
The fresh air is good for us
Our manager is proud.
Half-time we have a break.
At full time, we hopefully have won!

We are Aston Villa!

Sandy John Bulmer (10)
Hinstock Primary School, Hinstock

Great Britain

G reat people did great things.
R ightful say in parliament.
E veryone has the power.
A wesome monuments are built
T o honour our heroes.

B ritish pride has travelled the Earth.
R eal British pride and culture,
I s all around the world.
T owering hills and mountains, endless rivers and huge forests.
A nimals, so many and great.
I t is never too late.
N ow to visit us you can't wait!

Edward Lewis Bromley (11)
Hinstock Primary School, Hinstock

A Winter's Day

Lots of snowmen built today,
Put on your hat and gloves.
Snowflakes falling to the ground,
Everywhere is white.
Icicles hanging from trees and houses,
Snow lying on the ground like a white blanket.

But the snow is melting
And I am sad.

The snow has gone!

Lucas Gauntlett (7)
Hinstock Primary School, Hinstock

The Fall

Colours of autumn
Are gold, red, yellow and orange.
Sounds of birds tweeting
And rustling of the leaves.
The smell of wood smoke
And the feeling of cool air.
The conkers in their shells
Are protected with a hard spiky shell.
Inside is a smooth shiny conker.

Max Haines (9)
Hinstock Primary School, Hinstock

Winter

Winter is cold,
Some animals hibernate.
Children play snowball fights.
Water is frozen,
Roads are slippery,
Cars are crashing,
Icicles are sharp,
Winter is cold.

Toby William Irvin (8)
Hinstock Primary School, Hinstock

Amazing Acrostic Alliteration

A nnoying, angry, aging ants arguing about addition.
L arge lanky lions leaping lazily long ways.
P retty preening perfect peacocks pumping pathetically.
H orrible heartless hairy hippos happily hoping.
A wesome and amazing apes ambling and arguing.
B uzzy bouncy bumbly bees buzzing by blackberries.
E normous elephantine elephants eating eggs.
T en tipsy teddies tumbling topsy-turvy.

Brody Emile Wooding (10)
Hinstock Primary School, Hinstock

World War II

It's World War II!
Bombs exploding,
Machine guns firing,
Air raid sirens wailing.
As the days go on
People dying, children crying,
Mums worrying,
What's going to happen next?

Poppy Bulmer (8)
Hinstock Primary School, Hinstock

War

Bombs exploding everywhere,
Machine guns blasting fire,
Tanks rumbling across the ground,
Searchlights looking into the night sky,
Aeroplanes exploding,
Sirens screaming,
I'm terrified!

Ellie Clowsley (8)
Hinstock Primary School, Hinstock

All About Me

Into fashion,
Cute and sweet,
Very girly,
Delicate dancer
Make-up lover
Always fun,
A little princess.

Tabitha Gauntlett (9)
Hinstock Primary School, Hinstock

Kitten

K arate master,
I ntelligent animal,
T he cheeky one!
T iny teaser
E ndless playmate,
N aughty boy!

James Sale (11)
Hinstock Primary School, Hinstock

The Fall

Crunching leaves
As I walk along
The damp ground smells musty.
It's snowing leaves,
They float slowly, gracefully to the ground.

Jayden Holding (9)
Hinstock Primary School, Hinstock

Silly Sounds

Funky famous flamingos flapping funnily!
Busy bumbly bees buzzing by the blueberries!
Sad smooth snails sliming slowly sideways!
Happy hopeful horses hopping happily home.
Large lanky lions leaping like lemons!

Shannon Bailey (10)
Hinstock Primary School, Hinstock

War

Tanks blowing up,
Guns firing,
Exploding bombs,
Everyone screaming.
Will this ever be a happy place again?

James Tarrant (8)
Hinstock Primary School, Hinstock

Graveyards

We silently stand,
Waiting for bodies
To enter the coffins.
A collection of flowers is
Placed on us
For memories.

Wrought iron gates creak
Open and closed,
Like a person standing on a
Broken floorboard.

Ghosts as white as snow,
Sweep quietly around us.
Some of us have been knocked down
Because the ivy has strangled us.

The rough wind crashes onto us.
Spiders scurry around the
Moonlit grass.

Bats fly around the church's steeple.
Church bells ring for
The death of a loved one.
Church windows are covered
In bloodstained cobwebs.

We have been here ages
So quiet
So quiet
We rest in peace.

Lara Victoria Grove (10)
Huntingtree Primary School, Halesowen

Graveyards

The screaming gates creak open;
Like a person treading on a broken floorboard.

Galloping ghouls screech as if a crow had
Just been shot.
They cry out into the open
Darkness,
Asking for revenge.

Engraved gravestones
Are filled with messages from loved ones.
They wait for a dead body to fall down
To darkness and doom.

Silently bats glide about,
As if a farmer was trying to shoot them
With a gun.
They whisper to each other,
Their fangs clicking and chattering.

A blanket of red flowers dances in the
Strong and howling wind.
They shiver and hesitate,
But carry on dancing wildly.

A strange tranquil feeling of
Loss and despair spreads across the
Abandoned graveyards.

Bloodstained church windows are
Covered in silky cobwebs.
Ghostly faces - as white as snow -
Peer out,
Wanting to escape the cursed church.
So quiet,
So quiet,
The graveyard will rest in peace!

Amy Julie Garvey (10)
Huntingtree Primary School, Halesowen

The Storm

She swiftly sprints,
Across the street;
Searching for her next victim.
Plunders him with her almighty strength,
And runs before she is seen again.

She twists and turns,
In the screaming night;
Pleading for help,
But nobody comes,
Nobody ever comes.
She is angry now;
So very *angry!*

She cuts through grass,
Like a knife would cut through jelly;
And strikes down rooftops with just a single touch.
She is an assassin without a victim.

She's crying now;
As she slaps innocent buildings and shelters,
Like an angry girl who has just been dumped.
She's so alone;
And so sad.

She whimpers in the corner of the street;
Regretting her sins.
But,
You can't blame her;
She's all alone!

Jonathan Cook (11)
Huntingtree Primary School, Halesowen

HMS Victory

HMS Victory creeps through the water,
swimming like a swimming racer.
It throws cannonballs at its enemy,
while planning its next move.
To the water it will fly,
as its cannons never die.

Steven Ward (10)
Huntingtree Primary School, Halesowen

The Weather

Thunder is as loud as a lion,
He roars and growls at you.
He is a hot explosion
And scares you when you're walking down
The pathway.

Rain drips and drops at you.
Clouds are like sponges.
Slowly they squeeze themselves
And the little raindrops quickly fall to the
Concrete, hard ground.

The sun is a hot furnace,
He burns the Earth,
And will turn everyone
Into dark brown crisps.
He's like a big bully and will burn
Anything he likes.

The wind is a man with a big breath.
He blows the leaves
And makes them dance around
Everywhere,
All over the floor.

The snow is cotton wool.
She is soft as a furry cat.
She dresses the world in white.
The grass is green, suddenly it's white as a ghost.

Mona Abdo (10)
Huntingtree Primary School, Halesowen

TV

The TV jumps up and down, because the volume is too loud!
It must have a frown.
It shines up to the sky, that's how high.
It can talk as if it is you.

The buttons are shiny,
I clean them every day.
It stands on a stand like a hand on the arm of the sofa.

Joel Wyer (10)
Huntingtree Primary School, Halesowen

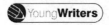

The Weather

He is a burning hot
Oil lamp which will never
Be put out.

Also he gets angry when
Kissing clouds get
In his way.
Sometimes
He disappears for an hour or two
Then silently creeps back out.

She is like icing sugar
And as white as a ghost,
She has slowly been scattered across
The frosty floor.
Slowly,
She melts but,
Then she quickly moves
To the next town.

He is as fast as a cheetah and
He howls as loudly as a crying dog,
Also he can rip trees out of the floor
And he can violently tear
Roofs off startled houses.

He is a dripping tap which will never stop
Also he causes chaos and destroys
Towns, cities and countries.

Jack Layton (10)
Huntingtree Primary School, Halesowen

Graveyards

Gravestones waiting to consume lives
Sleeping like old beggars,
Corpses in a never-ending sleep
Entwined with ivy.

The clock strikes twelve
Whilst the moonlight shines
And sings aloud,
A high-pitched sound,
The clock screams.

Coffins lined with bloodshot velvet,
Opened up by grave robbers
She pulls them into an early death
Impaled by a filthy tree.

All scavenging faces
Stare down at the early deaths
And think, *tea.*
Swoop down eagle-eyed
Feast!

The graveyard bellows and cries,
Cries,
Cries,
Cries with laughter
And gruesomely growls . . .

Vinnie Waldron (10)
Huntingtree Primary School, Halesowen

Grass

The grass is a musician as it
Plays a sorrow song.

Grass can live for one million years
And still be as green as an apple.

Grass is a flexible gymnast
Swaying all day long.

Grass stands as strong as can be
Like the world's strongest man.

Connor Preece (10)
Huntingtree Primary School, Halesowen

The Graveyard

A silver lit moon floats in the dark sky,
Watching over the city of stone.
Loud chimes ring out,
As the Earth claims its next victim.

Wrought iron gates creak open,
When two green eyes slip onto the path.
Like a dog she gazes at the crowd,
Huddled in the icy wind's breath.

A steeple towers over the packs of graves,
Dreaming of all the lost souls.
Footsteps crunch across the rocks,
Strewn across the church's shivering porch.

Graves lie as still as houses,
Choked by the way ivy wrapped around them.
Flowers curl up against them,
Attempting to keep warm.

Sounds of weeping fill the air,
As silhouettes glide through the frozen yard exit.
Slowly the shiny green eyes glint,
While they move in the moonlight to a pile of soil.
She wraps her dark tail across her face,
As she drifts to sleep.

Zach Elliott Jewkes (11)
Huntingtree Primary School, Halesowen

The Moon

The moon lights the galaxy
like a million suns.
It waits for its next victim
and then it runs.
It illuminates fog like a
sitting ghost.
It sits along the sea
like a flashing coast.

Will Eardley (11)
Huntingtree Primary School, Halesowen

Seasons

Trees yawn after their deep rest,
Tired wings swoop down to nest,
New beginnings wake up to the world,
Cries of hunger vanish quickly,
Like wind whisking things away.

Fun and laughter echo through the world,
As fierce as a bull,
The furnace in the sky
Billows down rays of fire,
Only to be caught in the wind.
He takes off his jacket from the heat from the sun
And smiles a big bulging smile.

Autumn is an old man,
His stick batters leaves from the trees,
His wrinkly face chases animals away,
His sly nature makes laughter disappear,
He is a fox chasing a rabbit,
Waiting to rip all hopes away.

Towns wipe away silky sheets,
Clouds whisk snow around the world,
All animals vanish,
Like owls swooping down to catch their prey.

Joseph Cresswell (10)
Huntingtree Primary School, Halesowen

The Graveyard

The graveyard is cold and dull,
With the crooked gate creaking,
And gravestones lying down and yawning;
Standing there all day through rain and bad weather,
Sadly they can't sleep; they have a job to do.

As the church bells wail,
The trees smile and laugh,
They've taken another life into their home,
Swallowed up bodies are never seen again;
Rotting under dead flowers.

All of them love Halloween so much,
They scare all the children;
The trees rustle their leaves,
Gravestones pull faces like clowns,
Ghosts lurk about jumping out at people.

Christmas comes, snow as well,
The church gets crowded with people;
People singing and praying,
Everything looks more lively;
With its white blanket,
But it is still as scary underneath.

Jessica Handley (11)
Huntingtree Primary School, Halesowen

Weather

The wind is an angry dragon.
He moves as fast as a cheetah,
And howls like a dog.
As he knocks over trees,
And lifts off the roofs of houses.
He roams the world
Freezing people
And destroying towers and cars.

As I fall from the sky,
And get closer and closer to the ground,
I freeze.
As I turn to snow,
I cover the whole roads in white.
As the children come out and,
Make snowmen,
But after a bit I melt,
As the children stay inside.

The sun is a fiery furnace.
He burns people's eyes as they look at him.
He helps the flowers grow,
And brings light to our day.

Dylan Rose (10)
Huntingtree Primary School, Halesowen

The Sea

The sea is a slow slithering snake,
Sliding up the bay,
Swallowing ships,
And eating people.

He runs to beaches,
And washes seaweed up onto the beach,
He poisons people,
He has some of the world's most deadly creatures,
Lurking in him.

He is as big as the universe,
He has lived for millions of years.

When he is angry,
He splashes people,
He floods beaches and cities,
And flies over people.

When he's happy
He is as still as a closed door,
He is as blue as the sky,
Asleep all day,
And awake all night.

Tammy Burgoyne (10)
Huntingtree Primary School, Halesowen

Weather

The rain is a huge tap.
Quickly he walks down your windows.
He pours down,
Like a waterfall is in the sky.

Snow is as soft,
As a bed of cotton.
Soon she will freeze her own fingers.
She is a white witch.

Thunderstorms are gunshots,
At war.
Loudly he booms
Like the clouds are playing drums.
Booming and banging across the sky.

The sun is a big red balloon,
In the sky.
She sizzles and spits in space.
She's a huge burning ball of fire.
Bad-tempered,
Bad-tempered,
As she always is.

Kirsty Smith (10)
Huntingtree Primary School, Halesowen

The Graveyard

In the moonlit graveyard,
In the night
The gravestones lean away from the church,
As they get strangled
By ivy.

The church glares at me
Playing its ongoing tune.
The tall bell towers
Tower over the huge graveyard
Like a giant over a man.

The people have their past
And only their past,
They sleep silently
But they never wake up.

The crows stare as
You go into the church.
When you come back out
They're still watching,
Watching,
Watching.

Jack Hubball (10)
Huntingtree Primary School, Halesowen

Rivers

A river is a snarling snake!
Every day and night,
Water goes flowing down the stream.
Just like a snake he hisses at you,
Ssssssss.

He strongly sneezes,
When something is thrown into the water.
While pushing it to the bottom,
He carries it away.

When the wind is strong,
A river twists, turns and flips over!
Every hour of the day,
Every day of the week,
Every month of the year,
Snakes head towards the sea.

Slowly, silently and softly,
He flows away.
And is never seen again . . .

Ellie-May Pallett (10)
Huntingtree Primary School, Halesowen

The Weather

The sun is a ball of fire,
Red and gold,
It shines in the sky,
Like a beautiful jewel.

It's sizzling like a sausage,
And burning like coal,
It makes you feel hot and warm.

The snow is a polar bear,
White and cold,
It's soft like fur,
Yet as cold as ice.

Snowflakes dance silently,
So calm and gentle.

The wind is a werewolf howling,
So loud and so fast,
It makes you feel scared.

It can be strong and powerful,
And blows in all directions.

Halimah Bibi (10)
Huntingtree Primary School, Halesowen

Christmas Tree

The Christmas tree is as green
As the Grinch,
And as prickly as a hedgehog's back.
The lights twinkle like stars,
In the night sky.
Baubles shine like gold, and
The bells sing like robins,
On a frosty morning.
And the ribbons wrap up presents,
As we wrap up as well.
Tinsel sparkles the whole of the tree,
And shimmers like moonlight.
But at the top the star stands like a soldier,
Saluting in mid-air.

Daniel Body (11)
Huntingtree Primary School, Halesowen

Snow, Snow, Snow

He falls on Christmas Day,
Hoping for children to play with;
He shivers all day,
Shivers all night,
Hoping not to be washed away.

Unluckily the next day,
Towns wipe away the silky sheet,
Leaving only ice to play with.

The snow queen appears,
Where has all the snow gone?
With a click of a finger
The snow reappears.

Snow is like Christmas, it comes and goes,
It's waiting,
Still waiting,
For next time,
Snow is also clouds but on the floor
Soft and white.

Shannon Stamps (10)
Huntingtree Primary School, Halesowen

The Christmas Tree

The Christmas tree
Is as spiky as a tree
Branch in the winter.
Baubles reflect like
Thousands of mirrors
In a circle.
Tinsel shines like
Cats' eyes.
Presents are wrapped up
As we wrap up.
Bells chime like bluebirds are
Singing in the winter.
Lights twinkle like stars in the night sky.
The star is like a soldier
Standing in gold clothes.

James Gordon (10)
Huntingtree Primary School, Halesowen

Weather

I steal hats
And crumple leaves.
I can take rooftops
And blow down doors.
I'm as fast as a cheetah.

I roar
And bang.
I am dark
And dull.
I can destroy trees with one strike.
I can harm you!

I climb up high
In the sky.
I have a ferocious temper.
My temper will never end.
I can burn.
I climb down the sky for the night to begin.

Bethany Whyley (10)
Huntingtree Primary School, Halesowen

Weather

I am a burning oil lamp
Every day I watch the world go by
But sadly when night comes,
I silently disappear,
Sometimes when black rain clouds
I may not be there the next day

I am a never-ending drip of water;
Drip-drop, drip-drop.
Sometimes I make floods
But if the temperature drops,
I freeze and turn into snow.

I am like icing sugar flying all over the floor;
White and slippery
When the ground is full of me,
I slowly make my way to the next village.

Britney Saunders (11)
Huntingtree Primary School, Halesowen

Your Only Friend At Night

In the late night hour,
He comes and smiles.
He sits there all day,
Silently waiting for the darkness.

He watches you,
While you're fast asleep.
That big rock in the sky,
The moon, he waits for you.

She lights him up in the dark,
The sun, the light in the day.
He is as cold as a winter's day,
Freezing the night away.

He follows us,
Slowly all year round.
Never leaving,
Never disappearing.

Caitlin Lemon (11)
Huntingtree Primary School, Halesowen

The River

The river is a snake,
Quickly I go down the lane,
Like a cheetah trying
To chase his prey

Roughly I crash,
Into a small brown rock,
Sometimes I get twigs and leaves,
Thrown at me.
Sometimes I'm quick,
Sometimes I'm slow.
Twirling and twisting,
Sliding from side to side,
Down the lane.

I go from north to south
Never go east to west,
And slowly I fall into the sea.

Hadeel Mohammed (11)
Huntingtree Primary School, Halesowen

The River

She is a slimy snake
That swallows anything in her way,

Blue as the sky,
And full of life.

Trees are watching her every move,
Moonbeams light her way,
The grass is howling
While the flowers are sleeping,
Leaves dance away.

Foxes lurk around
Being careful to not fall into her trap,
Looking for their midnight snack.

Heading south
Towards the sea
Where her friends wait for her,
On her never-ending journey.

Leah McKenzie (10)
Huntingtree Primary School, Halesowen

Waterfall

I am a gush of water
Sometimes I can be big
Sometimes I can be small.

I can make a rainbow
Which will never go
I can make a splash.

I can destroy boats
Make people fall to their deaths.

I will never freeze up
As I am always running
I will never run out
I travel the world
Joining packs.

I can be slow
I can be fast
I am like a sideways stream.

Jordan Edwards (10)
Huntingtree Primary School, Halesowen

The Holly Bush

The prickly ends,
Slice the berries,
Like a chef in the kitchen,
Slicing cherries.

The holly bush,
Moves in the wind,
Like a girl,
On a swing.

The holly bush,
Sways side to side,
Like a woman waving,
At the seaside.

The holly bush whistles
Like a man,
Picking fresh,
Emerald-green thistles.

Brooke Gwinnell (10) & Phoebe Connop (11)
Huntingtree Primary School, Halesowen

Stars

Stars twinkle like a lit
Christmas tree,
Shooting star sprinting across
The sky like an athlete.

Stars watch the world
Transforming,
It's a piece
Of the moon breaking off.

Stars stroll across the
World to their next destination,
Like a Sat Nav guiding it
Through the galaxy.

Stars are a never dying object,
They have no grave
And no tomb.
They have space though.

George William Cox (10)
Huntingtree Primary School, Halesowen

Volcano

V iolent volcanoes start to erupt.
O nly minutes till the city gets covered with a thick layer of ash.
L imited time to get out.
C hunks of ice fall off the volcano like houses falling out
   of the sky.
A lert! Alert! The ash is falling down, down, down to the
   city below.
N owhere is safe, everywhere dangerous.
O pening up, the volcano erupts.

Alice Ray (7)
Kinlet CE Primary School, Kinlet

Volcano

V ery silently the volcano starts to shake.
O range oozing lava like orange juice waiting for me to drink.
L ots of lava dropping like rain, making a flood.
C ooling, crashing, oh my,
A sh alert! Atchoo! Atchoo! Oh no, atchoo!
N ever open a window if you hear a volcano.
O verflowing memories of that day keep on coming back.
    I wish it had never happened.

Kloe Pearce (7)
Kinlet CE Primary School, Kinlet

Volcano

V ery hot lava exploding out of the top of the volcano.
O nly volcanologists know when the volcano will erupt violently.
L ives are being lost.
C rackling noises come from the boiling hot lava.
A mbulances come like lightning to rescue people.
N ation is being destroyed with anger.
O verflowing smoke making the city dreary.

Brandon Wyatt (10)
Kinlet CE Primary School, Kinlet

Volcano

V olcanic eruptions are dangerous, they can kill you.
O range hot lava like orange juice with washing up liquid.
L ava breaking out of the volcano, making a flood.
C radling people in the airport, it is gridlocked.
A sh clouds in the sky, millions of them.
N oisy volcanoes erupting like thunder.
O verflowing lava from the volcano.

Joseph Field (8)
Kinlet CE Primary School, Kinlet

Volcano

V olcano violently erupting.
O ozing hot lava.
L ava can suddenly come out of a volcano like a river.
C an you escape from a volcano splurging out hot lava.
A s rocks crash down?
N o one can survive.
O nly the volcano is left.

Amber Byrne (7)
Kinlet CE Primary School, Kinlet

Volcano

V olcano, volcano, oh rumbling volcano.
O verflowing red hot bubbly lava.
L ovely you are.
C rater so big it's cool.
A sh filling the air, how beautiful.
N oisy bangs, ear aching.
O ften erupting.

Jacob Loynton (8)
Kinlet CE Primary School, Kinlet

Volcano

V olcanoes vomit lava very, very, very fast.
O utstanding oozing orange lava rocketing off.
L oud bangs like gunshots! *Bang! Bang!*
C louds of gas, smoke and ash drop down.
A lert volcanologists 24-7.
N obody goes near except volcanologists watching.
O verflowing lava, all different colours - fascinating.

Emma Field (10)
Kinlet CE Primary School, Kinlet

Volcano

V iolent volcano spurts through the cracks.
O ozing out, lots of lava overflowing.
L ava spurting out of the crater.
C louds black as coal in the air.
A larms ring out warning of the disaster.
N othing left, everything's destroyed.
O pen the door and run for your life.

Ross Quickenden (9)
Kinlet CE Primary School, Kinlet

Volcano

V olcanoes spurting out lava as if they were throwing up.
O ozing out lava as if it was tomato juice.
L oud booming noises like thunder in the sky.
C louds of ash coming towards me.
A sh is everywhere.
N othing left, everything gone.
O nly the volcano is left.

Daniel Hilton-Hill (7)
Kinlet CE Primary School, Kinlet

Volcano

V olcanoes vomiting like someone being sick.
O range lava spouting out of the crater.
L ava squirting out of the crater.
C raters open up like rain clouds.
A lert alarms going off, people panic.
N obody goes near the volcano erupting.
O verflowing lava sliding down volcanoes like a flood.

Jessie Egginton (7)
Kinlet CE Primary School, Kinlet

Volcano

V olcanoes erupt like a rocket.
O ur planet will die.
L ips open, boiling hot lava bursts out.
C ards are made in sign of danger.
A nd I got saved by a helicopter.
N o one else got saved, only my family.
O ne day the volcano stopped like traffic lights.

Sophia Robinson (7)
Kinlet CE Primary School, Kinlet

The Eclipse

Moon
I move across the blinding sun
I have never stopped nor never won.
The sun has never lost to me
Although to her I'm like a tiny pea.

Sun
I am like the queen of space
The planets spin all over the place.
When the planets spin they make me dizzy
At least they keep me super busy.

Earth
I live in a place called the Milky Way
I don't see an eclipse every day.
the moon graciously orbits me
maybe one day he won't be so funny.

Space
Before I came with a big *bang!*
Now all of those planets just hang.
Pluto is a tiny dwarf ant
This is what the others chant.

A Star
I move across the horrendous sun: *Swoosh!*
Sometimes I have a little fun.
Like watching kids wish on me
As I shoot so fast you can't see me.

Ellie Rowton (10)
Mesty Croft Primary School, Wednesbury

The Family Of Planets

Mercury is burning hot.
He is as small as a pea.
Mercury needs a friend, always.
He needs someone to look out for him.

Venus is as poisonous as a snake.
She is as hot as a ball of fire.
Venus runs as fast as a cheetah.
She is as bright as a star.

Earth is boiling from its core.
She lives in the huge Milky Way.
Her sister, Venus, is beautiful.
If Earth died right now, no one would live.

Mars is red as a juicy cherry.
Huge dust storms everywhere on him.
An enormous valley runs through his veins.
Volcanoes everywhere erupting.

Jupiter, the dusty planet.
He is as huge as a mountain.
A red spot tickles his head day and night.
Moons here, moons there, moons simply everywhere.

Saturn spins so fast, you can't see him move.
He is as light as a feather.
He is as yellow as a banana.
His rings are made of cold ice.

Uranus is as blue as the ocean.
He spins super fast on his side.

Neptune's clouds surround him every day.
He is a small gas giant.

Pluto is as small as a speck of sand.

Elisha Bagdi (10)
Mesty Croft Primary School, Wednesbury

My Wish

I saw the stars in the sky,
They all make wonderful shapes,
But then one thing caught my eye,
But what on Earth was it?

Of course, it was a shining, shooting star,
I thought I'd make a wish,
The star was racing away,
So I'd better make it quick.

I wished that I could go to space,
I thought it would not come true,
So I made my wish quietly,
And then something happened too.

There it was in space - *wow!*
A meteor came livid,
It was trying to find somewhere to crash,
One landed, *bang, bash, bang, bash.*

Next I saw the melancholy moon,
Then the bully - the sniggering sun,
The poor moon could not cope,
Maybe I could give him a bit of hope.

I saw where our planet lives,
With all of its brilliant friends,
Of course it was the Milky Way,
I was tired so down I lay.

Now I've ended my great journey,
It has been fantastic but long,
I have had a great deal of fun,
But now my poem ends here so
I had better run!

Abi Joy Glover (11)
Mesty Croft Primary School, Wednesbury

The Hole

A hole of death . . .

It savagely sucks all life from a star.
Never beginning, never ending.
Sneaking past stars, creeping past galaxies.
A hole of death.

A hole of cunning . . .

Cleaning the universe, like a perfectionist.
Never beginning, never ending.
Eating things up, a huge appetite.
A hole of cunning.

A hole of despair . . .

When it sucks a star away, it laughs.
Never beginning, never ending.
Laughing and killing, everything dies,
A hole of despair.

A hole of sombreness . . .

After everything dies, it silently cries.
Never beginning, never ending.
All on its own, nothing to do.
A hole of sombreness.

A hole of wonder . . .

A stunning star, blows up as it's created.
Never beginning, never ending.
Its blind eye never seeing.
A hole of wonder.

The hole.

Ryan Jones (11)
Mesty Croft Primary School, Wednesbury

Our Solar System

It all started with a big *bang!*
As the small hard pieces hung
Floating in the night sky
Then all the planets started to form
Finally, all the planets were born.

All the meteors floated around
In the Milky Way galaxy
Stars were banging into each other
The black hole is as black as death.
The Rover goes around Mars, lonely and sad.

The moon was all alone like a lonely seed.
Then finally, someone was there
He was feeling happy: he wasn't alone.
Then he started treading on him
And he jabbed a pole in him.
The moon started to cry.

It was a big, scary astronaut
His boots left thick footprints on him
Now he has gone, he is alone again
He will just sit and wait for someone to come again.

Will he ever have a friend again?

Bethany Molineux (11)
Mesty Croft Primary School, Wednesbury

A Melancholy Moon

As I looked outside my bedroom window,
I saw the moon; a lonely, melancholy, depressed moon.
Not a sound to hear; just a sigh of depression.
Always being bullied by the hot, powerful sun.
No visitors anymore
Not since Neil Armstrong stabbed him with a flag.
Then he left him all by himself.
Satellites and planets pass by
Not talking, ignoring his tears.

Chloe Lane (11)
Mesty Croft Primary School, Wednesbury

Up There

Up there, Venus winks at me.
Up there, Jupiter blows.
Up there, Pluto sings joyfully
And I see some UFOs.

Up there, I see the Mars Rover.
Up there, I hear Saturn cry.
Up there, the stars make a clover.
Then I see a star passing by.

Up there, geysers explode with a splash.
Up there, the moon is Swiss cheese.
Up there, I see a flash
And then I hear Neptune sneeze.

Up there, I see stars dancing.
Up there, they have a race.
Up there, Saturn has a ring
And I can see our moon's face.

Up there, I see gas giants.
Up there, the sun says, 'I'm hot!'
Up there, it's simply science
And that's all that I can spot.

Masie Griffiths (11)
Mesty Croft Primary School, Wednesbury

The Moon

It's as lonely as an orphan with no one to talk to,
It's like a god watching from above the atmosphere,
A sphere-shaped observer of the orbit of the sun,
The start of a huge universe has just begun.

Through the years and through the days of loneliness
No one comes to see the wonderful sight,
Not a lot to do, but a lot of shining light,
The moon lets out a cry; it has no one to talk to.

Liam Davies (10)
Mesty Croft Primary School, Wednesbury

Bang!

Bang!
Metal and rock joyfully raced and spat
They twisted and turned in the super sky
They jumped and flipped like an acrobat.

Bang!
Rocks fell, tumbling down the never-ending path.
Falling, falling down, down, down.
Playing, giggling, 'Ha, ha, ha,' laugh, laugh, laugh!

Bang!
They play together, never break
They close in tighter every day
What is that? Could it be a lake?

Bang!
I'll call her Venus, goddess of peace
The small red one Mars god of war
The inside core as warm as a fleece.

Bang!
The galaxies are now alive
The Milky Way is born
And as busy as a beehive.

Chloe Webb (10)
Mesty Croft Primary School, Wednesbury

Sparkling, Shooting Star

The shooting star was overjoyed to grant wishes.
It went skimming across the sky, waving at.
Passing satellites and planets with near misses.
It granted wishes for free.

They do everything to keep people glad.
Sometimes with some wishes they go mad.
But sometimes peoples' wishes are very bad.
Then they get so furiously sad.

Farhana Begum (11)
Mesty Croft Primary School, Wednesbury

Journey To The Moon

The melancholy moon cried as he didn't have a friend.
It was like he was the only person in outer space.
The lonely moon sighed as he orbited planet Earth.

The moon felt dejected as no one came near.
Sadly, the moon watched the shooting stars playing around him.
It was like he was invisible to other planets.

Satellites by planet Earth seemed to ignore him.
He was just a loser in space.
No rockets came near;
It was a lonely life for him.

All planets stopped and stared
Did not ask him to play.
No astronauts came to stay;
All they did was take photos.
He feels like he's being used by people on planet Earth.

All he is, is a ball of ice and rock
That is why he has no friends.
He wishes a star could grant him a wish.

He wishes he had a friend in space.

Shahana Uddin (11)
Mesty Croft Primary School, Wednesbury

The Moon's Life

The moon sighed as it was without friends.
The moon said, 'Earth is proud of its atmosphere.'
The melancholy moon turned its head away.
The moon looked to the dark as it shed a tear.

Boom! went the rocket as it hurt the moon.
As the moon saw someone it found a friend.
When the rocket had left, the moon waved goodbye.
Then he noticed he was lonely again.

The moon looked at the other moons sadly.
The moons joked, laughed and bullied the moon.
When he blocked the sun, he was filled with joy.
His back was a burning prune.

Conor Ireland (11)
Mesty Croft Primary School, Wednesbury

Stars

The stars danced excitedly with joy,
It's a sight anyone would enjoy,
They chased each other all day long.
Singing one of their happy songs.

They come out at night; they hide at day,
It's such a shame they cannot play.
Twinkling brightly in the night,
Shining, shining extremely bright.

Making pretty constellations.
Pictures from every nation.
As the day comes, they fade away,
But they will come out another day.

My poem sadly ends here.
As the night draws to a clear,
They might come again: they might never,
But I will remember this day forever.

Abigail Elizabeth Brain (11)
Mesty Croft Primary School, Wednesbury

Super Space And Brilliant Beyond

The midnight moon as cold as the Arctic.
Asteroid belt soaring between Mars and Jupiter like an eagle.
Shooting stars dance together across the midnight sky.
The moon is a giant ball of delicious cheese.
That explodes with flavour on your taste buds.

The Mars Rover sadly strolls across the dark rusty surface of Mars.
Gravity is as strong as the world's strongest man.
Satellites watching everything that happens.
Happily recording as it goes along.
Making sounds as it goes along all the time.
The stars smiling, shimmering, sparkling and shining while lighting up the
dark night sky.

The big bang was as loud as a clap of thunder.
A UFO soaring slowly glowing green in the starlit sky.
Neptune is blue like the dark blue ocean.
An eclipse as beautiful as a baby butterfly.

Chloe Henn (10)
Mesty Croft Primary School, Wednesbury

Space Race

The space race has begun.
As the planets speed around the sun.
The planets move with a cheetah's pace.
Who will win this first space race?

Jupiter takes the lead.
He shows all the greed.
The planets don't want to crash
They know they will be trashed.

Neptune and Jupiter work together.
To throw Venus into the sun
And she burns Venus' fragile bum.
They're into the last lap of the race.

It's between Jupiter and Neptune.
No one else is anywhere near.
All the rest fall back in fear.
Neptune is triumphant again.

Daniel Jack Fielding-Adams (11)
Mesty Croft Primary School, Wednesbury

Journey To The Moon

The melancholy moon cried as he didn't have a friend.
It was like he was the only person in outer space.
The moon watched and stared as the shooting star danced in
the dark sky.
Battered by asteroids,
Laughed at by the sun and planets,
Satellites ignored the old, battered moon crying,
No more rockets passing to play;
They just stopped and stared.
Planets passed by; all they said was, 'I don't care.'
His heart lifted as finally Planet Earth smiled at him with kindness.
Now all the planets stopped and talked.
The cheerful moon danced as it came from its dark sleep,
All the shiny stars stopped and played;
All they said was, 'Yay!'

Lewis Richards (11)
Mesty Croft Primary School, Wednesbury

The Satellites

The satellites are sparkling,
Like a shiny golden key,
With their flat, smooth panels,
With a joy that filled me.

Transmitting signals day and night,
But they're always lonely,
No one to talk to,
Never showing they're happy.

When one suddenly breaks down,
Its brothers and sisters weep,
And while all this happens,
The Earth just falls asleep.

A satellite's final journey,
Is falling,
Falling, falling, falling,
Until death.

Kai Marriott-Shaw (11)
Mesty Croft Primary School, Wednesbury

The Life Of The Moon

A tear dropped from the moon's eyes
As the rocket took off
It was lonely once again
The moon sighed at the Earth
And Earth smiled back at it.

Happily the moon smiled back at Earth
As his heart lifted from a deep depression
The sullen feeling inside of him exploded - *boom!*
The moon cheered at this happiness.

Strangely there was one thing annoying the moon
The beaming rays of the sun were burning him
He was slowly disintegrating to a crisp
And he waved goodbye to Earth.

Bradley Elks (10)
Mesty Croft Primary School, Wednesbury

Space Is Here

Space is a dark, deserted place far, far away.
With billions of stars shining, dancing all around.
Space is here, space is there,
Space is simply everywhere.

The moon is a ghostly galleon upon the midnight sea,
Neptune, as cold as the Antarctic, feels depressed and lonely.
Space is here, space is there,
Space is simply everywhere.

Timeless, immense, stretching out from a deep, dark, black sleep.
Swallowing new and old worlds as they come and go.
Space is here, space is there,
Space is simply everywhere.

Exciting new galaxies exploding:
Dazzling fireworks every second.
Space is here, space is there,
Space is simply everywhere.

Meghan Harris (11)
Mesty Croft Primary School, Wednesbury

The Arrival On Mars

I travelled to mini Mars
To try and find an alien.
I heard a voice behind a rock
It peeked around a corner and shouted!

A monster, green, gloomy, glowing with only one eye,
Travelled towards me as slow as a snail.
I thought it would destroy me
But I was wrong: it was friendly.

When it finally reached me
It hugged me with delight.
I asked the creature, 'Do you want to be my friend?'
It smiled at me with excitement:
My heart lifted.

Jenny Morris (10)
Mesty Croft Primary School, Wednesbury

The Life Of A Shooting Star

This is the life of a shooting star.
It is as fast as the fastest car.
The star was ecstatic zooming past lumps of rock.
Beaming boastfully, the star was burnt by the sun.

The sullen star soared through the universe,
Suddenly, *boom!* It crashed into Pluto.
The scorched star was shattered and scattered.
As it floated all through the solar system.

His soul was unleashed; he was happy.
He was now free to roam around space.
He was so cheerful that he could see his friends.
This is a wonderful story of a star.

Declan Hill (10)
Mesty Croft Primary School, Wednesbury

Contentment!

Some say contentment is pink like candyfloss.
Others say it's yellow like the sun!
You may say it's as colourful as a rainbow.
I just think it's really fun!

Some say contentment tastes like the creamiest ice cream.
Others say it's like the yummiest pud!
You may say it's as juicy as strawberries.
I just know it tastes really good!

Some say contentment looks like a spring glade.
Others say it looks like a bright smiling sun!
You may say it looks like a stunning butterfly.
I just think it's really fun!

Some say contentment smells like the sweetest pollen.
Others say it smells like pine wood!
You may say it smells like beautiful red roses.
I just know it smells really good!

Molly Rose May Vann (11)
Queen's CE Junior School, Nuneaton

Fairies

These little people, so bold and small,
With little baggy shirts coloured green,
That have a belt, with a horn.
With dirt on their faces,
They will always look a disgrace.

They live on Hipple Top mountain,
And use blackbirds to travel
To gardens near and far,
They will be a sight to see and hear.
As they travel through the air
You would hear their bells
Which hang from their little red hats.

They shelter under pine trees,
To stay dry,
And they cry and cry when other fairies die.
But mostly they laugh and play games in the grass.
So if you see little lights on the ground,
It may not be glow worms,
It may be fairies playing tig and other games.

So don't say you don't believe in fairies
Because if you don't
One may surely die.
So believe!

Emily Barrow (10)
Queen's CE Junior School, Nuneaton

In Class!

When Miss Moore is stressed
The whole class is in a mess
Pencils are on the floor
Right next to the door
She trips on the floor
Miss Moore stands, she also demands
'You naughty little scrams!'
Everyone's acting like a pest
Life in class is a test
Miss Moore needs to take a rest!

Adam Siddat (9)
Queen's CE Junior School, Nuneaton

My Brother

My brother is such a naughty boy
When he's angry he throws his toy
He's not a baby, in fact he's ten
So he should know better but then
At the church hall he did shout and scream
Ripping up artwork, he's no dream
Just because he didn't get his own way.
Oh boy, what a lousy day.

But then on another day he can be so kind
So generous, an absolute joy
On these days no toys he throws
No shouting, no screaming, no artwork destroyed
On days like this I love him and he loves me
And I say what a fantastic day.

Catherine Jasper (7)
Queen's CE Junior School, Nuneaton

My Dog Mac

My dog is called Mac
He is short and very black.
Mac chases cats down the yard
Pounding his paws very hard.

He's got a bed in the kitchen
By the window on the floor
Where he sits and begs for more.

We take him for walks in the park
If he sees a bird he likes to bark.
He chases the squirrels round the trees
Then rolls about in the leaves.

When he gets home he'll lie on the floor,
Close his eyes and loudly snore.

Charlotte Dalton (10)
Queen's CE Junior School, Nuneaton

Poems Are Great

P oems
O n different topics.
E nthusiastic.
M ums and dads love poems
S o you can love them too!

A bsolutely astonishing.
R eading is good for your minds.
E ven learn things from them.

G reat for your learning.
R eading poems is such fun.
E xtraordinary sentences
A nd unique
T itles.

Karla McKeown (9)
Queen's CE Junior School, Nuneaton

Recycling

R ecycling is to help the world.
E ach thing needs to be recycled.
C ans are in the bottom of the red box.
Y ou need to help the world.
C ans can be made again.
L ook out for rubbish.
I n bags please.
N ot there in the red box.
G o and recycle and get new things.
    Please, please, please recycle
    Thank you!

Hannah Rose Jones (8)
Queen's CE Junior School, Nuneaton

25th Of December

Wake up early to see,
Lots of presents under the tree.
Sing, dance, have lots of fun,
If you're lucky you can have a bun.
Wrapping paper all over the floor,
No one can get in from the front door.
Christmas dinner is yummy to eat,
While lots of family we wait to greet.

Chloé Downs (10)
Queen's CE Junior School, Nuneaton

Love

A special world for you and me
where's a better place to be?
There's nothing I'd rather do
than spend it with a person like you.

Whenever you're hurt with bruises and scars
I'll take you to your star to make you feel . . .
Love is . . .

Davina Vallabh (11)
Queen's CE Junior School, Nuneaton

The Aliens

A liens came down to Earth,
L ying there, waiting to surf,
I s this really happening?
E veryone screaming for help,
N ow everyone, please don't shout,
S omebody please get them out.

Alicia Patel (11)
Queen's CE Junior School, Nuneaton

If I Had Wings

(Inspired by 'If I Had Wings' by Pie Corbett)

If I had wings I would
pounce like a kangaroo to the
moon and watch over the Earth.
I would gaze upon the beautiful
nature down below me.
I would be able to hear the chirping
of the birds whilst singing a lullaby.
The animals would be able to crawl
around me and know that wasn't their prey.
My wings would help me to spring
across the diamante sky whilst
looking at the sparkles that have
been thrown across the black sheet of felt.
I would be able to soar across
the sky as I would see
the stars that are
rockets that have
been frozen in space.
I would dream of
travelling to see all
the cities, all the people
and be able to speak all
the languages of the world.

Abigail Bradley (10)
Roberts Primary School, Dudley

A Night Of Doom

One giant shining eye watching all.
Wolves howling, cats prowling.
The trees stand and stare menacingly at all that pass by.
Bats like flying beasts waiting for their prey to come.
The woods like a maze of deep, dark, doom.
Holes like never-ending chasms of doom.
Cats and foxes were thieves stealing lots of food.
Shadowy figures were ghosts walking relentlessly.

Matthew Ward (11)
Roberts Primary School, Dudley

If I Had Gills

(Inspired by 'If I Had Wings' by Pie Corbett)

If I had gills I
would soar across the ocean
and taste the salty water.
I would feel the water
splash over me like a
champion swimmer.
I would dive deep down
like sliding down a slide
and listen to mermaids sing.
I would look around for any
passing predator.
I would leap out of the water
like a cricket jumping
in the meadows.
I would jump out to
fresh air.
I would dodge all the shooting nets.
Then I would see all the animals
that have never been seen before.
A million diamonds dance across giant blue sheets.
A giant green shell diving in a green bath.
A small red rock scuttles across the bed of blue water.

Molly Emery (10)
Roberts Primary School, Dudley

The Haunted Mansion

The front door was a doorway to Hell,
The ghostly old mansion was as bare as a prison cell.

In the night shadows were creeping upon the walls,
And out came the eerie and deadly ghouls.

As the clock struck twelve the mansion flooded with darkness
It was a giant wave crashing to the ground so rough,
The statues were waiting, staring like they were so tough!

The cobwebs were as big as bats hiding in the darkness
So creepy, and as the sun rose once again,
The ghost town disappeared as the house grew sleepy.

Jamie Langley (10)
Roberts Primary School, Dudley

Personification Poem

The wind blowing your thoughts away
Is the torrent of darkness.
The rusty eyes that stare into your thoughts.
The cat that looks at you,
Always waiting to pounce.
The sound you hear
When the moon reads the wind's thoughts.

The trees look over you
Like you're their slave.
The wind tries to stop the moon
Reading its thoughts.
The cat that looks at you
Is as silent as the wind.
The rusty eyes that you see
Are the eyeballs of thunder.

As you gaze at the stars
They start to dance in the sky.
The trees upon you
Are filled with death and hunger.
The squeals you hear
Are the children playing in your head.

Aaron Jones (11)
Roberts Primary School, Dudley

The Magical Night

Tick-tock, the day goes by,
The night is a knife, silent but deadly.
Tick-tock, the night turns on,
Eerie trees stand tall like guards protecting the night.
Tick-tock, the night goes on,
Rivers run and spit like a baby in the silver glitter light.
Tick-tock, I carry on through the black,
The stars are winking at me from the jet-black sky.
Tick-tock, the hours draw on,
Leaves soar through air when there is no wind.
Tick-tock, the moon comes out to play, the sun has gone away,
The trees whistle in the breeze.

Lindsey Emma Air (11)
Roberts Primary School, Dudley

The Spooky Night

The graveyard is an unused battlefield
When the sun dies down
And the moon dances up
The graveyard comes alive.

Leaves brushing,
Laughing like cackling old ladies.
Owls hooting
At the sight of black cats screeching.
Sleeping wolves steal the moonlight
After every breath.

Shadows screaming at the sight
Of grey figures moving.
Trees' trunks have horror faces
After seeing ghosts peeping out of their graves.

The moonlight disappears
Like water down a drain.
The sunshine lights up the sky
Like a light bulb
And the spooky night is lost forever.

Maia Shillam (10)
Roberts Primary School, Dudley

Night-Time

The night is a dark void covering the land,
Cloaking the world in a soft duvet.
The moon transforms from shape to shape
From full moon to new moon like the cycle of life.
Shadows prance and shadows dance throughout the silent night.
'Oh no! We must go!' they say for dawn is on the rise.
The darkness walks and the darkness talks
Throughout the eternal night.
The world sleeps and dreams about waking up in the morning
About the wondrous adventures its creatures will have.
Weird shadows stop and stare at the glittering gold moonlit rivers
That shimmer like the stars.
They touch and feel but whenever they do
The gold is shattered and reverts back to water.

Samuel Acheampong (11)
Roberts Primary School, Dudley

If I Had Gills

(Inspired by 'If I Had Wings' by Pie Corbett)

If I had gills I would swim to Florida
like a torpedo and see the wonderful creatures.
I would feel the colourful coral
as a crab on the sands.
Swish.
Diving in the water as the smell of the sea
hits me like a heat wave.
Dipping in the water I would taste the salt
like a whale collecting plankton.
Eyes staring into the blue
as I wander through the depths.
Gills as shiny as a white cat in the moonlight.
I would hear the seagulls screeching as
I swish through the sea.
As I swim into the deserted mine
I'd see fragments of gold.
Diving into the grass as I go into space
I would bungee jump off the highest canyon
into the depths below.

Daniel Smith (10)
Roberts Primary School, Dudley

The Night

The night sky was silent and quiet,
The stars looked like a pot of gold,
The webs were shining and exquisite
It looked like they had jewels and pearls on them.

The moon drifts to Silver River to sleep,
The shadows are like a blackbird in the dark,
The moon lights up the thick black night,
The fog listens as it passes by.

The street lights stand there like a statue,
Shining on the floor,
The leaves dance in the dark,
The moon overlooks and brightens up
The wind is a cheetah.

Jack Chater (11)
Roberts Primary School, Dudley

If I Had Gills

(Inspired by 'If I Had Wings' by Pie Corbett)

If I had gills I would
swim elegantly through the
deepest of oceans, and discover things
that man could never dream of.
Swish!
I would shoot, like a torpedo listening
and gazing across the ocean, like a herd
of elephants being poached by the enemy.
Swim!
Coral would brush against me like brown
shrivelled leaves on an autumn branch.
The scaly creatures of the sea
would look upon me thinking
what an extraordinary crossbreed I was.
Sound!
I would listen to the friendly crustaceans
of the sea, snapping away at the seaweed
with its white rotting cells.

Harry Beardes-Hancocks (9)
Roberts Primary School, Dudley

Snow Valley

All the glittering stars
Guide people at night
While the merry snowflakes
Dance as they
Fall from the sky.

As the freezing and frightening forest
Wanders through the valley
The colossal green trees look at me
When I am walking past.

As I sit down
The stream that is as blue as the sky
Dreams as it flows by.

Bethany Owen (10)
Roberts Primary School, Dudley

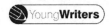

A Night

A thick black silence shadowed the sun
Everything was turning to silver
Glittered stars danced beside the moon
The brilliant moon was like a silver spoon.

Shadows weirdly shadowed the moonlight
The silent wind whispered like soft music in the dark clouds
The silver grass reached up on tiptoes to meet the moon
Hooting owls were car horns of the twilight sky.

The silver river whispered softly to the moon
Things watching like eyes of mystery
The river was sleeping silently
Soon the sun would appear.

Night was silently melting
Dawn was swiftly appearing
Silver stones were turning yellow with the sun's light.
The sun was the new magical mystical ruler on the throne.

Laura Elizabeth Hawkins (10)
Roberts Primary School, Dudley

The Creepy Graveyard

Silence. Nothing dared move.
The graves glistened in the moonlight
Like ghosts appearing in the shadows,
The wolves growled.
Their scary yellow eyes were two bright tea lights.
The statues stared, looking like they were ready
To put up with many types of fights.

Silence. Nothing dared move.
The tall, bending trees shivered as a wave of wind
Was cast over them,
An owl swivelled his head round like a revolving door,
Rats scuttled across the floor.

Silence. Nothing dared move.
The moon was a light bulb casting a ghostly light,
Shadows wept where no silvery glow could see,
But still, nobody knows about the ghosts that are free.

Alex Yorke (11)
Roberts Primary School, Dudley

Night

The sun goes down, the moon goes up,
The pavement is the path to Hell,
Every child snug in their bed,
The diamonds rise, hidden by the dark clouds,
The moon is as white as a ghost,
The black cat yells in the moonlight,
The sun goes down, the moon goes up.

The monstrous demon roams around in the sky,
The darkness is a demon's face,
The gloomy ghostly shadows scurry around the streets,
The wind screams as the moon shows its face,
Time stops as the poltergeist jumps,
The trees are as tall as death itself,
The demon bats fly in the sky,
The sun goes down, the moon goes up.

Josh Graham (11)
Roberts Primary School, Dudley

Personification Poem

Twinkling snowflakes
dance in the night sky.

The bright twinkling stars
listen to the blowing wind.

The burning fire is as hot as a boiler
and listens to trees blowing.

The dancing robin sits in the blowing tree
as super sparkling snowflakes dance around him.

The dark night sky
listens to my dreams.

Edward Holland (11)
Roberts Primary School, Dudley

Nights

Street lamps flashing like moonlight beams touching the Earth.
Rain pouring as swiftly as the fastest person in the world.
Rivers waiting, waiting for daylight to come for the animals to drink.
Street lights are soldiers lying in the street,
As rain pours like tears coming and falling from a person's face.
A river is a giant's puddle of tears flowing.
Street lamps are car lights smashing the road.

Regan David Hudson (11)
Roberts Primary School, Dudley

Personification Poem

The robin teaches
The snowflakes to dance.
As the stars tell the church bells
To listen.
And the stream
Teaches the frost how to dream.

Phoebe Timperley (11)
Roberts Primary School, Dudley

Home Time

Big old buildings
Swaying high up in the air.
Children running out,
Teachers shouting, 'Take care!'
You can hear children chatting about
Things they have to do.
You can smell the bread
From the bakery.
Can you smell it too?
I can feel my muddy clothes
That's one of the things
I have to do
Now school
Is over
We can enjoy it too.

Olivia Wilson (10)
St Benedict's Catholic Primary School, Mancetter

In Our Town

In our town,
Snug houses and
Tall, towering buildings fill the street.
In our town,
There are places to go,
And people to meet.

In our town,
Playful children skip
Along the rough, pebbly road.
In our town,
Worn-out workers take their trip
Past barking dogs and factories.

In our town,
A deep, musky smell
Fills the air and atmosphere.
In our town,
Colossal, billowing chimneys
Puff smoke from their smiling mouths.

In our town,
The chilly evening breeze
Sweeps through my hair.
Our town
Is the place to be.

Anouk Sequin Mary Smith (10)
St Benedict's Catholic Primary School, Mancetter

VE Day

Flags waving frantically
In the air,
Wind blowing through my hair.
As I was forcing myself
Through the wind
When I nearly
Bumped into a tall building.
It nearly touched the sky.
Busy people shouting,
Some were shy.

Lily Grace Farr (10)
St Benedict's Catholic Primary School, Mancetter

VE Day

It's VE Day,
Yee-hay!
I'm at the town hall today,
To celebrate VE Day.

Eating sweets,
As my mother eats.

Beautiful decorations glimmer and shine,
For it is a day of nine.

My father enters,
With a big smile on his face
We have all thought about him,
And yet he does not look dim.

When he comes up to us
We remember the time that we stayed with him.

We eat candyfloss,
We sing along to a butterfly song,
As the day goes along.

Ryanne Howard (9)
St Benedict's Catholic Primary School, Mancetter

The Moaning Mill

The moaning mill,
Has bursting, bustling people,
Bursting out of its full mouth.
As I think to myself,
What a dusty, dark mill,
With very rusty limbs,
The moaning mill.

The moaning mill moans day after day.

The moaning mill
Spits out smoke violently
They sky goes grey,
And just lays.

The moaning mill moans day after day.

Eden Edney-Jones (9)
St Benedict's Catholic Primary School, Mancetter

At The Fairground

I wonder what I can smell?
Candyfloss they will sell.
Mad music I can hear,
I will never fear,
What will I see,
For all is not about me.
Ice cream I will eat,
Right down to my feet.
Groaning grown-ups are so soft,
Even if they live up in the loft.
Chatting children are so fun,
How fast can they really run?
Popping popcorn is so sweet,
Always need a tasty treat.
Dogs are barking,
I keep marking,
Where they're barking.

Alice Brierley (9)
St Benedict's Catholic Primary School, Mancetter

The Fun Of A Fairground

I could smell the popcorn,
Mixed in with petrol of generators.

People at the fairground
With big tall hats,
Dark black suits,
Angry little dogs
Wanting to go for a walk.

You could see the big,
Red buttons of the controls
When you sit on the carousel
Little bumpy horses,
Spinning round,
And round.

You could hear little birds,
Sneaking down to grab some popcorn.

Owen Morris (9)
St Benedict's Catholic Primary School, Mancetter

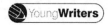

Sandy Beach

Chaotic children running around,
Ebony boats sailing,
Across the wavy sea,
Happy people playing games,
Wrestling people with their chains.

Sea weedy, sea greeny-blue,
Bricked buildings along the sea's edge,
Screaming babies after food,
Barking dogs of all breeds,
All getting annoyed because they're stuck on leads.

A pointy steeple high in the air,
Fluffy clouds searching the sky,
Eating ice creams on the beach,
Bright lamp posts,
On the edge of the sand.

Ellie Clover (9)
St Benedict's Catholic Primary School, Mancetter

Smoking Chimneys

The chimneys smoking,
People heading to their houses,
Huge buildings in the sky,
Jolly people jumping high.

Dogs barking and playing too,
The big grey pavement going through,
The huge shopping queue.

The old brown gate blocking your way,
Unless you're willing to pay.
A big strong man blocking the gate,
I think he's been lifting a weight.

The fog on the windows blocking my view,
As I call a window cleaner too.

Ross Paton (10)
St Benedict's Catholic Primary School, Mancetter

The Evening Town

As the bitter sweeping chimneys
Clouded over the city

The drunken men reeking of tobacco
Twirled and twisted across the street.

People merry and well fed,
Drifted out of the theatre without a care in the world.

The slightly buzzing lamp post
Lit the way as the persevering pandemonium the pilgrims caused.

The smooth immaculate theatre is out of place,
Next to the dark, roughly weathered houses.

The devious barking dogs snap at your heels
As you come by.

Lauren Cook (9)
St Benedict's Catholic Primary School, Mancetter

VE Poem

Red flags flapping,
People saying, 'Hooray!'
Everyone jumping up and down,
Smoke going up into the sky,
As people dance all about.
Dogs barking,
Beautiful buildings decorated,
Army men coming back from the war,
You can see the smoke,
From far away
Is in the sky
Can't you see?
Joined up house, beautiful decorations.

Jarrad Wood (9)
St Benedict's Catholic Primary School, Mancetter

The Fair

You can smell,
Burning burgers,
Broken rides,
Smoke from magicians,
Cleanness of brand new won toys,
The meter of madness is full to the top,
Children pulling their parents to go on the best ride,
The handyman cleaning the red sauce from the roof,
The roller coaster swirling around like it's alive,
You can feel the shaking wind touch your face,
There are cola bottles on the floor,
The wind blows in your face,
And knocks the apple core out of your hands.

Sarah Read (9)
St Benedict's Catholic Primary School, Mancetter

At The Fair

You can smell,
The sweet smelling candyfloss,
Through the cold windy air,
As I taste the crunchy popcorn,
Sticking to my hair,
I touch the cold shiny metal on the carousel,
Can you feel it as well?
I love watching the horses swerving around,
They go up,
They go down,
I can hear the children playing around,
How I enjoy walking around,
I'm sure I'll go back the fairground.

Marie Horsley (9)
St Benedict's Catholic Primary School, Mancetter

A Day At The Seaside

The sea is splashing up on the shore,
A bird with a black claw.
Some people are shouting,
Babies are panting,
Dogs are barking,
People are harking.

Buildings are big,
People are having a jig.
People are going in and out,
In a pout.
Rowing boats on the shore,
Some are poor.

Paige Batty (9)
St Benedict's Catholic Primary School, Mancetter

Good Friday

Millions of people being crazy,
Running to lines,
Pushing and pulling to the front.
Quite a few crazy dogs
Jumping up and down.
The taste of candyfloss,
Sweets flying into my mouth.
Hilarious street performers trying to get a bit of money,
Loads of people starting a riot!
People breaking it up.
People looking for money,
Children going on treasure hunts.

Jasper Wilson (9)
St Benedict's Catholic Primary School, Mancetter

VE Day

Hooray, hurrah, the war is at an end.
Hooray, hurrah, England has a new friend.
Hooray, hurrah, no more terrible guns to fear.
Hooray, hurrah, no more shedding a tear.
For the screaming and shouting can no longer be heard.
And as for the tragic death in the war,
No one has even hit the floor,
Hooray, hurrah, the party can begin,
Hooray, hurrah, as true as our word, we win,
Hooray, hurrah, a story we can tell,
To our aunt, uncle and niece,
Hooray, hurrah, England can live in harmony and peace.

Phoebe Hargreaves (10)
St Benedict's Catholic Primary School, Mancetter

Tiny Street

People are running out of their houses
to get some treats.

The shopkeeper is busier than ever
in his tiny little van.

You can smell the smoke puffing from the
ginormous chimney.

The children are playing in the middle of the
path being very careful.

You can hear dogs barking
for miles and miles.

Alex Freeman (9)
St Benedict's Catholic Primary School, Mancetter

The Roaring City

Walking through the streets at night.
A cold chill up my spine.
The street looks as if it's roaring out,
Trying to give me a fright.

Poor people sleeping out in the cold,
The dark skies covering the moon,
Blocking the glow out of sight.

The roaring city will soon yell for you,
So be aware when you are in the dark . . .

Argh!

Oliver Hargreaves (10)
St Benedict's Catholic Primary School, Mancetter

At The Sea

As the bright shining sun,
Shone in my eyes.
With the sandy slopes,
And the shining blue sea.
The children splashing in the water,
And the parents groaning.
I heard the howling wind,
And the sight of boats,
Floating in the sea.
The sight of the
Waves crashing into the water.

Massimo Cunsolo (9)
St Benedict's Catholic Primary School, Mancetter

Fun At The Fairground

I can see clowns doing tricks,
Actors behind the scenes eating a Twix.
Magicians making people amazed,
They look at the fairground and are dazed.

Adults walking dogs,
No one feels down in the bogs.
Children on a roundabout,
People eating candyfloss no doubt.

Fun at the fairground all day,
Hooray!

Nathan Dittman (10)
St Benedict's Catholic Primary School, Mancetter

VE Day

I taste the layer of black smoke,
I hear a frog croaking,
I touch a metal tank,
I see soldiers on wooden planks.

I hear people crying for their sons.
I see people eating jam buns.

People crying, people smiling
For some it's goodbye forever
And they will never float like a feather
316 living on but will die later on.

Jack Cook (9)
St Benedict's Catholic Primary School, Mancetter

A Day At School

School children come out of school.
While waving goodbye to teachers.

Dark dusky clouds start emerging
High houses looking down, goodbye they frown.

Cities full of big, bold buildings,
Chuff-a-puff chimneys, every school child.

Children wave, 'Take care,'
They say goodbye to their school friends.
The day ends with a happy heart of joy.

Ellie Gough (9)
St Benedict's Catholic Primary School, Mancetter

The Fun Of A Funfair

Lively dogs smelling hot sausages,
Excited people tasting sausage rolls.

The amusement of clowns making people laugh,
And the blowing of trees in the breeze.

A plain playing field with nobody on,
That's a lonely playing field with nobody on.

A boingy bouncy castle with people watching,
With a farmer on the field flocking the sheep.

James Grimes (10)
St Benedict's Catholic Primary School, Mancetter

Sunny Sandy Beaches

The sunny shining sand,
Being played in with hands,
While the chaotic children,
Begging to go in the weavy windy water,
Big bashed boats rolling over the slight wind,
Dogs dozing on the sand,
Also the steeple
The biggest in the land.

Blake Kent (9)
St Benedict's Catholic Primary School, Mancetter

Grandma's House

In the deep dark woods,
Covered in pin rosebuds,
Sat old Grandma's house.

In a light blue coat,
You'd take a note,
The red around her lips,
She'd have a glass of water and take a few sips.

When you went inside, you wanted to hide,
For on the walls there were not jewels,
Instead children's toys.

The hairs on your neck,
Would be dripping with sweat,
At the sound of her croaking old voice.

Oh, and the wardrobe,
The freaky old wardrobe,
Would moan and groan right through till morning.

Out the back,
Was an old grey sack,
Inside was a lovely pup.
Everyone wants to stay and play,
Until Grandma eats you all up.

Freya Asker (10)
St Lawrence CE (VA) Primary School, Napton

The Forest

As I walk along the forest floor,
I can hear the birds singing their song in my ear,
The colourful leaves fly through in and out the trees,
Whilst the bed of leaves dances around my knees,
The wind whistles and blows my long dark hair,
As the sticks blow about in mid-air!
It's getting dark in the deep, dark wood,
All that's left is a little brown mouse,
That little brown mouse finds a nut,
And the nut is good!

Charlotte Paynter (10)
St Lawrence CE (VA) Primary School, Napton

Snow

The leaves dance around my feet,
Whilst blackbirds in mid-air tweet,
Snow-white sheep bleat,
As I skip along the frozen concrete.

Suddenly I feel a bluster of snow,
Biting off my frozen toes,
Making white marks on the end of my nose,
Whilst curtains in warm snug homes, close;

I wish I could be all snug,
Sitting under my snuggest rug,
Then I see all the miniature bugs,
Sitting with their hot chocolate mugs!

Then I seem to be on my road,
Where all the people have seemed to have goed,
Because they knowed,
That it had snowed!

I rushed up to my front door,
The knocker had been covered with thaw,
I looked at my white wellies on the frost floor,
And wished that it would snow some more!

Charlotte Wilkins (11)
St Lawrence CE (VA) Primary School, Napton

Tornadoes

She catches me and hurls me up,
She wraps her ferocious arms around me,
She twirls like a ballerina up and down,
She breaks my bones and crushes my home,
She picks on small or large things,
She comes at a fast speed,
She scares people away,
She wrecks the place when she spins over,
She is a horrible bully to the people,
She is not a nice person to go and talk to,
She might come at any time,
Beware, Tornado is coming . . .

Madison Collins (10)
St Lawrence CE (VA) Primary School, Napton

My World

My world would be packed with dogs and cats,
Listening to music while eating bats.
I would have loads of friends,
There would be no such thing as bends.
For my world is mine to design.

I would be famous, a pop star with loads of wins,
I would rule my kingdom with a thousand boxings!
My people would love me more and more,
If anything hurt me it would not feel sore.
For my world is mine to design.

Everyone could be royal,
And eat sausages on a coil.
I would stay up all night,
Stay up with no light.
For my world is mine to design.

I would play cowboys and Indians everyday,
Eating pizza, non-stop play.
It's called New England, welcome everyone,
Feel free to play, dance in your knickers.
For my world is mine to design.

Elliot Newland (9)
St Lawrence CE (VA) Primary School, Napton

Evening

The last of the rosy sunset waves goodbye
And fades away into a velvety darkness
Littered with diamonds that are
Billions and billions of stars.

The stream that runs by is of silver,
By the large white moon's gleaming light.
The only sounds are the giggling and chattering
Of the stream and the low hum of insects.

The knee-length grass is still and full
Of wild flower buds and silky moths
The warm air smiles but her breath does not stir
Everything is slow, sleepy, settling down to rest.

Katie Line (11)
St Lawrence CE (VA) Primary School, Napton

The Grotto

From the grotto,
From the old, dark, eerie grotto,
Comes a sound;

The sound of a footstep
Smacking the floor of the grotto,
The dank floor of the grotto,
The damp floor of the grotto.

From the grotto,
From the old, dark, eerie grotto,
Comes a smell;

The smell of evil,
Distorting the air of the grotto,
The clammy air of the grotto,
The ombrophilous air of the grotto

From the grotto,
From the old, dark, eerie grotto,
Comes a deathly silence;

The silence which comes
When a demon is roused . . .

Catherine Jessett-Brown (11)
St Lawrence CE (VA) Primary School, Napton

My Mind

My mind
Is like a Ferris wheel
For it goes round and round and round.
Dreaming all day long in a planet of its own.
It's almost like a clone of me
But just how I want it to be.

No rooms to tidy, no beds to make,
Just go to sleep or bake a cake.
My mind is mine,
Mine to keep, mine to know
Not for you, no, no, no!

Isabella Cuffaro (10)
St Lawrence CE (VA) Primary School, Napton

The Graveyard?

What happened at the graveyard?
The wind howls through the winter trees
Belonging to the graveyard up ahead.

What happened at the graveyard?
The skeletons sleep in their crumbling graves,
And the gloomy church looms over the silent graves.

What happened at the graveyard?
When I walk through the graveyard gates I can feel
The maggots slithering through the skeletons down below.

What happened at the graveyard?
Sometimes you can see ghosts with blood-red eyes
Wandering through the graveyard.

The graveyard
The graveyard
Watch out,
You're next . . .

Matthew Molloy (10)
St Lawrence CE (VA) Primary School, Napton

Fear

Fear is a cruel person.
She takes away your joy.
Stealing all your happiness, just for herself.
She sits in the corner,
With her head tucked away,
Thinking of all the worries inside.
Crawling up your chilled spine
Whispering her worries into your ear.
Her glistening eyes trembling
Full of sadness and loneliness.
A moth-bitten sack hooked on her back
Following getting bigger . . . and bigger,
Until she can't carry it anymore.
Fear is a cruel person,
But only because you let her in.

Beth Ovens (11)
St Lawrence CE (VA) Primary School, Napton

The Warm Winter's Eve

Winter
Winter is cold, winter is dim
I love snowmen
I love hot milk when I get home.

Winter
I make a fire and turn on the TV
Then snuggle up next to my mum
And then I go to sleep with my teddy!

Winter
I love opening prezzies on Christmas Day
I love roast dinner with turkey
Then I go sledging until I rest my head.

Winter.

Amy Leigh Boby (10)
St Lawrence CE (VA) Primary School, Napton

Puppies

Puppies hug
Puppies love
They play today.

Puppies eat their
Dinner as fast
As a shooting star.

Puppies are as
Cuddly as a
Teddy bear and
They like me to
Brush their hair.

I love puppies,
They love me!

Katelyn (10)
St Lawrence CE (VA) Primary School, Napton

Mew

Mew is playful,
Mew is joyful,
Mew is helpful.

Mew

Mew is washable,
Mew is playable,
Mew is helpful.

Mew

Mew is a fighter,
Mew is loveable,
Mew is the best!

Mew!

Rhys Newland (9)
St Lawrence CE (VA) Primary School, Napton

A Bully

A bully, neither a name nor a place,
neither an animal nor creature . . .
but - a small word that describes such a big thing!
A girl or boy, whose eyes have been shielded
and taken for bad.
A bully always has a reason for the way they are
good or bad,
you should listen.
A bully may look tough!
but on the inside they're as weak as a kitten.

A bully gave into the problem;
they're a bully to themselves.

Bring out the big bad bully!

Georgia Edginton (10)
St Lawrence CE (VA) Primary School, Napton

The Chocolate Muffin

My chocolate muffin is:
A chocolate mountain,
A spongy wonderland with a stream running through it,
A puffy autumn leaf,
A chocolate rock,
An eye popping sensation waiting to satisfy your taste buds,
A crumbling building that melts in your mouth,
The reason you get up in the morning,
And . . . it's all mine!

Charlie Thurlow (10)
St Lawrence CE (VA) Primary School, Napton

Music

Songs can be sad,
Songs can be bad,
Songs can take a lot of time,
Like it's taking to write this rhyme,
Melodies can be strong,
Melodies can be long,
Lots of people use it,
It's called music!

Tia Hudson (11)
St Lawrence CE (VA) Primary School, Napton

Spring

Spring takes over the world like a peaceful God.

The colourful leaves float around the wonderful world.

The colourful leaves beneath your feet dance around in the air like a magical river.

If the colourful leaves mix together, they will be a beautiful butterfly.

Danni Louise Kimberley (10)
St Lawrence CE (VA) Primary School, Napton

Story Poem

Once upon a time there was an old lady,
She invited little children and even babies,
I bet you're thinking she's friendly and kind,
But no, you're definitely on the wrong line.

She invited everyone to her house,
And then would say, 'Do you want a mouse?'
All the little ones would be so confused,
But they didn't know she was nasty and cruel.

Then one day, it was a boy,
All happy and excited, full of joy.
He came in the house and sat on a chair,
He asked, 'Can I please have a pear?'

She said, 'No dear, have a mouse.'
He said, 'Ha-ha, I've already been to this house!'
She ran away from the place,
It was like she was having a race!

Umair Munir (9)
Ward End Primary School, Birmingham

Really I Did

I saw a monkey making bread,
I saw a girl composed of thread,
I saw a towel one acre square,
I saw a meadow in the air,
I saw a rocket walk a mile,
I saw a pony make a file,
I saw a blacksmith in a box,
I saw an orange kill an ox,
I saw a butcher made of steel,
I saw a penknife dance a reel,
I saw a sailor twelve feet high,
I saw a ladder in a pie,
I saw an apple fly away,
I saw a sparrow making hay,
I saw a farmer and he says too,
That these strange things were all quite true.

Aneeka Akhtar (9)
Ward End Primary School, Birmingham

Everybody's Body

My school has a *head*,
The cliff has a *face*,
The needles have *eyes*,
Walls have *ears*,
A river has a *mouth*,
A bottle has a *neck*,
Treasure has a *chest*,
A book has a *spine*,
A clock has *hands*,
The sea has a *bottom*,
A table has *legs*,
You're the bees' *knees*!
The bed has a *foot*.

Joseph Brunn (10)
Ward End Primary School, Birmingham

Spring

Spring is coming,
Birds are humming,
What a sweet noise,
Chicks are hatching,
Plants are growing,
What a nice day!

It's spring,
It's getting hotter and hotter every day,
It's spring in an all new way,
People laughing in the outside world,
Let's step into it today!

Wajiha Naz (9)
Ward End Primary School, Birmingham

What Am I?

I am small, and not everyone notices me,
I am innocent, and yet I am dominated by the world,
I am floating all over and get blown around,
I am in a different destination all the time
And don't know where I will be next,
I am invisible to some, yet noticeable to others,
I am not an unpleasant smell and cannot smell anything.
There are lots of me around you,

What am I?
A speck of dust.

Yumna Ayaz (10)
Ward End Primary School, Birmingham

What I Want

I want to fly,
Be able to float,
Go into space and see planets.
I want to be in a real football match,
I can score goals and my friends are watching.
I want to draw,
Make art and invent things.
But most of all,
I want to be a good friend.

Sonia Hussain (10)
Ward End Primary School, Birmingham

Mom Helps

Mom you're a wonderful mother,
So gentle, yet so strong,
The many ways you show you care.
Always make me feel I belong.

You're patient when I'm naughty,
You give help when I ask,
It seems that you can do everything,
You're the master of every day.

Hafsah Iqbal (10)
Ward End Primary School, Birmingham

Cricket Season

The cricket pitch is awoken by the gargle of the gardener's truck,
The dust is sneezing because of the pungent paint as white as snow,
The stumps wake with the *whack, whack, whack* of them being knocked in,
The ball is finally picked up after a long uncomfortable sleep through the
winter months.

The anticipation of the crowd waiting for the all-in-white players to walk
smartly on the pitch,
The ripping of the pads in the changing area alerts the smart serious
umpires to emerge from the tunnel,
The atmosphere in the changing area is as tense as a rubber band,
The ground erupts as the players walk on the pitch,
The wind created by the bat and the *clump, clump, clump* of the ball hitting
the ground,
The roar of the crowd as a super six is scored and the *flick-flack* of the
scoreboard as the century is scored.

But now all is silent as the game is over
And the pitch, ball, bat and stumps fall asleep,
Wondering when they will see action again.

Benjamin Smith (9)
Webheath First School, Webheath

Springtime Animals

The squirrel's alarm clock is the sound of the fluffy snow melting quickly,
He bobs along like a bouncy beach ball
And he checks his breakfast treasures hidden under the rambling roots
Where the ants are scattered around like broken glass.

The colourful birds are perched in the tall tree,
Tweeting the joyful song of spring.
Their beaks are like pointy knives,
Ready to strike at the wriggly worms
Who like to wiggle around under the soggy earth.

The green grass grows for the lovely lambs to lick,
The newborn lambs start to feed from their mothers
And learn to walk with their unsteady legs,
Which are like a broken chair.

Stephen Vaughan (9)
Webheath First School, Webheath

Springtime

The dainty, dancing daffodils
Are waking up
They are yawning too
Their petals are a lion's mane
With their trumpets alerting the morning.

Baby animals are being born
Chicks, piglets and lambs too
They are trampolinists leaping around the field
The chicks are chirping, the piglets are snorting
And the lambs are bleating.

Easter eggs are very tasty
You see the children munching merrily
Crunch, crunch, munch, munch,
The Easter Bunny delivers them all
With their beautiful colours showing off.

Amelia Pearce (8)
Webheath First School, Webheath

Easter

The dainty, delicate daffodils
Bloom open like the
Sun rising from its sleep.

The delicious, chocolatey eggs
Relax lazily on the
Hard, wooden table.

The bouncy, fluffy bunnies
Hop gently with their white legs
And swishy tails.

Jasmine Bwail (8)
Webheath First School, Webheath

Easter Time!

Baby animals are being born
Lovely little lambs leaping like gymnasts through the field.

Trees standing tall, showing off their beautiful blossom
Daffodils yawning and stretching.

Easter eggs sleeping lazily in the Easter Bunny's tough wicker basket
As the Easter Bunny hops happily.

Liam Hunt (9)
Webheath First School, Webheath

Golden Sunshine!

Stop and look this way!
Hot, golden sunshine
Stunning as I look
Wow! It's so beautiful

Tell your neighbour Dave
Come outside and be brave
At least come out for a minute
Or maybe two

Ice cream is so yummy
On a sunny day
Make sure it does not melt
Or you will ruin your belt

Get the blue swimming pool out
And give your friend a shout
Come on out, it's sunny
Let's splash and play about.

Layla Williams (7)
Whittington CE Primary School, Whittington

Rain

R ain dripping from the clouds
A nd the weather gets wet.
I nside we are dry.
N one of it will stop.

William Neilson (8)
Whittington CE Primary School, Whittington

My Family

I love my family so much
Rachel is very pretty.
I love my family so much
Opa is an artist.
I love my family so much.
Oma wears rosy red lipstick.
I love my family
Jack has a teddy and never lets go of it.
I love my family
Mummy's fascinated with make-up.
I love my family
Daddy is a workman.

Hollie Edwards (8)
Whittington CE Primary School, Whittington

Donkey Kong - Jungle Beat

D onkey Kong beats Cactus King
O h so powerful
N icks bananas
K ingdoms
E ver so strong!
Y ummy, yummy bananas

K icks baddies
O n track
N asty baddies!
G ood at swinging on ropes.

Oscar Jumar (7)
Whittington CE Primary School, Whittington

Cowboy

C owboys coming to town
O n black horses
W ith their shotguns
B ang! A gun is fired!
O h no, someone's dead!
Y eah, it wasn't me!

Jason Reevey (7)
Whittington CE Primary School, Whittington

It's Raining

I sit listening and watching.
T he rain has started.
S ounds loud on the glass roof.

R unning down the windows in rivers
A nd everyone outside is getting wet.
I like walking in the rain.
N ot without my coat and wellies though.
I n and out of puddles.
N othing is more fun.
G et out, get wet when the rain starts.

William Evans (8)
Whittington CE Primary School, Whittington

Sunshine!

Golden, bright, hot sun
Rising sun, nice to see you
Boiling, beautiful sun
We love to play with you
Sparkling, lovely, shiny sun
We love you
So bright, so hot
Beautiful, shiny, stunning sun
Stop and look this way
Golden sun look at me!

Holly Owens & Freya Ellis (7)
Whittington CE Primary School, Whittington

Football

F antastic football!
O ut of this world!
O range balls in the snow.
T he whistle blows - off we go.
B alls zooming around like planes.
A ll the fans chanting players' names.
L iverpool is my favourite team.
L ove football, the best game I've ever seen!

Josh George Darley (9)
Whittington CE Primary School, Whittington

Ice, Ice

Ice, ice!
Stop there is ice,
Ice is on the way,
Watch out!
Shut the curtains,
Shut the door,
Ice is on the way,
Ice is freezing,
Ice is hard,
Watch out!

Jordan Joseph (8)
Whittington CE Primary School, Whittington

Snowy Day

Snow is as soft as silk,
White is like a swan or milk.
Ice so cold it freezes your fingers,
As if you have put your fingers in an icy pond.
Snow looks like someone has laid a soft, white and comfy blanket
On the Earth.
Birds cheep sweetly as they try to find worms hidden in the snow.
Butterflies and bees have gone to hibernate.
It looks like the plants have just said goodbye.
I'm going to bed.

Cecily Evans (8)
Whittington CE Primary School, Whittington

Wake Up!

Wake up, wake up
Give yourself a shake up
It's a sunny day
Let's go out and play today
Because it's a happy day
Because it's a happy day
The birds are singing and the bluebells are ringing
It's a happy day!

Alexander Young (6)
Whittington CE Primary School, Whittington

Outside

Come outside
See the lovely sunshine
You can have an ice cream
It will be your favourite flavour
Strawberry, chocolate and blueberry
You can have a gorgeous sunbathe
The sun is really bright
Golden like a big fireball
You can go outside in the swimming pool
You can hear the birds singing.

Daisy Hodnett (7)
Whittington CE Primary School, Whittington

Breathtaking Thunder

Break!
Thunder makes you wake
Powerful thunder makes you feel terrible
Makes you feel unbearable

Tell your neighbour Dave
Don't scare yourself, be brave
Stop!
It's coming.

Argh!

Phoebe Davies (7)
Whittington CE Primary School, Whittington

My Dog Casper

C asper is my dog
A ffectionate
S oppy, he always licks me
P layful, he is still a pup
E xcitable, always happy to see new faces
R etriever, he is a Labrador.

I love my dog Casper!

Lucy Cupitt (8)
Whittington CE Primary School, Whittington

Icy Ice

Icy ice, *stop!*
There is ice white
Ice on the road, *stop!*
Ice is bad.

A man said, 'It's very slippery outside.'
He was called
George.

Ivory Hickman (7)
Whittington CE Primary School, Whittington

Eva, Can You Teach?

(Inspired by 'Gran, Can You Rap?' by Jack Ousbey)

Eva was in the kitchen, she was eating a peach
When I tapped her on the shoulder to see if she could teach
'Eva, can you teach? Can you teach? Can you Eva?'
She swallowed her gulp and said, 'Are you a beaver?
I'm the best teaching teacher this world's ever seen
I'm a tip top, slip slap, teach, teach, queen!'

Jessica Charmley (7)
Whittington CE Primary School, Whittington

Lovely Sunshine

Lovely sun, nice and bright!
Golden hot sun in relaxing blue sky!
Huge and dangerous so never go near it,
Otherwise you will die!
Make sure you keep away from the sun!
Cyprus, nice and hot, you can go there
On a lovely holiday!

Eryn Reid-McCarthy (8)
Whittington CE Primary School, Whittington

Sunny Day

Quick, come outside, it's a sunny day
Come outside and then you'll see.

The sun is hot and soothing
Come with me and then you'll see.

The sun is shining,
Let's get the swimming pool out, *ssspppllash!*

Isobel Dawe (7)
Whittington CE Primary School, Whittington

My Cat Phoebe

P hoebe is my very special cat.
H er fur's black, white and soft.
O val green eyes stare up at you.
E very day she has the same routine: eat, sleep, eat, sleep.
B ut sometimes she plays just like a kitten.
E very day is a good day when she is on my lap.

Matthew Collins (8)
Whittington CE Primary School, Whittington

Hurricane And Rain

Run, run as fast as you can
or you will get sucked up forever
Shut your door and your window
or you will get wind in your home
You will suffocate
Everybody will go screaming to their homes.

Horace Remfry (8)
Whittington CE Primary School, Whittington

Food

F ruit is healthy for you.
O ld food goes mouldy.
O ranges stop you from having a cold.
D uck is nice in a spring roll.

Chloë Tomlinson (8)
Whittington CE Primary School, Whittington

Snow

Icy snow falling down,
Making people go outside,
It's cold out there,
Everybody's screaming there,
See - scream, scream, scream!

Roan Huggins (8)
Whittington CE Primary School, Whittington

Snow

Put on your coat
Keep yourself warm
Snow is coming
Snow is crunchy
Snow is snowmen.

Matthew Jones (7) & Ethan Edwards (8)
Whittington CE Primary School, Whittington

Swimming

I like swimming
It is as fun as ever
You swim back and forth
I like front crawl the best
It is fun when you know how to swim.

Todd Davies (8)
Whittington CE Primary School, Whittington

Butterflies

Butterfly, Butterfly, fly through the air,
Flapping your wings without a care.
Land in the trees and on the flowers,
Dodging the raindrops in the April showers.

Saffron Aston (8)
Whittington CE Primary School, Whittington

Little Hedgehog

Little hedgehog in the breeze
Walking slowly through the leaves.
He's in the forest
On the ground,
Hardly making any sound.
He's making a hole
For hibernating time,
And he's even making
His own rhyme hog, frog, dog . . .
He's playing games at the beach.
He's looking for a friendly leech.
He finds food
When he's in the mood.
He likes breakfast because it's sweet
And it keeps his mind off his smelly feet.

Noah Taylor (7)
Wilmcote CE Primary School, Wilmcote

Pussycat!

Pussycat in the bush
Trying not to rush.
Creeping, creeping round and round,
Trying not to make a sound.

Sneaking, sneaking in food,
Also treats when it's in the mood.
I think it's kind of funny
When you tickle its tummy.

On a hot summer's day it's lying in the sun
It's lying in the sun because it thinks it's fun.
It doesn't like water so don't try.
Don't put it in the bath or it'll cry.

Molly Gwynne (7)
Wilmcote CE Primary School, Wilmcote

One Fairy Tale

O nce upon a fairy tale,
N owhere without colour.
E veryone looking happy,

F airies especially.
A wonder awaits me,
I n a fairy tale.
R unning I see a deer, male
Y oung me,

T rying to see,
A fairy tale I see in me.
L oving it, I find out it's a fairy!
E very year she comes to tea.

Ann-Marie Calvert (9)
Wilmcote CE Primary School, Wilmcote

Mint Choc Chip

M an, ice cream is nice to eat,
I sometimes think it's a treat,
N ever live without ice cream
T ell me that you love this thing!

C an you eat ice cream when it's sunny?
H ave you had flavoured honey?
O wners never let you eat it,
C an you sneak one out of the freezer?

C hocolate bits is the best,
H ave you tried it in a test?
I n the summer it cools you down
P eople love it around the world.

Sabina Romano (9)
Wilmcote CE Primary School, Wilmcote

Summer

J une is sunny outside
U p, up in the sky the sun is shining.
N o dark clouds in the sky.
E njoy yourself in the summer.

I can enjoy myself in the summer.
S ummer is fun.

S un, you can play in the summer.
U nder your umbrella in the sun.
N o rain in the sky in the summer.
N ow you can eat ice cream.
Y ou can swim in the swimming pool.

Emily Cockram (8)
Wilmcote CE Primary School, Wilmcote

Animals

A ntelope and ape
N aughty newt nabbing your cape
I guana and mouse
M eerkat in your house
A ttacking everyone and everything
L unging and biting
S nakes slithering all around.

Animals all around
They like to bound
Jumping, leaping,
Running from cars that are beeping.

Rhys Duncan (9)
Wilmcote CE Primary School, Wilmcote

In Space

S pace is black and big with lots of
P lanets and spaceships swirling round.
A steroids landing on planets and
C lear view to see the Earth from
E verywhere around.

Hamish Huxley-Edwards (8)
Wilmcote CE Primary School, Wilmcote

Football

F ootball fun everywhere I look, vuvuzelas, people cheering
    England on.
O h no Germany have scored, 1-0 to Germany.
O oh, Lampard has been fouled, it's a penalty to England,
    goal, Gerrard has scored.
T eams cheering from different countries, go! Go! Go!
B ands playing famous songs.
A ction all over the pitch.
L oads of people in the crowd, about one thousand people.
L ines fading on the football pitch. The pitch is a disgrace.

Jacob Robinson (9)
Wilmcote CE Primary School, Wilmcote

Ice Creams

I ce cream is yummy in your tummy.
C ream is clean on your ice cream.
E nd or bend on the floor or by the door.

C old is good, east or south.
R unny in your mouth and melts quickly.
E gg flavour is yucky but it looks lucky.
A pple or raspberry is the best of all.
M aple syrup is the sweetest of all.

William Humphreys (7)
Wilmcote CE Primary School, Wilmcote

Ice Cream

I ce cream is cold and runny,
C ould you eat it when it's sunny?
E verybody loves it.

C ream is an ingredient you put in it,
R eally it does not make you fit,
E ating it on the beach,
A pple flavour or maybe peach,
M any people buy it!

Emily Browne (8)
Wilmcote CE Primary School, Wilmcote

Animals

A nimals in herds, animals in groups.
N othing's better camouflaged than a snake in a loop.
I n the jungle it's warm as a tin of soup.
M assive animals, small animals, any shape or size.
A mazing creatures jump out in your surprise.
L ithuanian jungles are very, very hot so watch out for
those sneaky flies.
S avage animals are everywhere so watch out for the big guys.

James Messenger (9)
Wilmcote CE Primary School, Wilmcote

Pussycat

P retty little pussycat purring away. Happy little pussycat day by day.
U nusual little pussycat swimming away.
S hy little pussycat, don't be afraid.
S undays are always sunny, better find some shade.
Y ahoo! Hip, hip, hooray, it's my birthday.
C rawling up the bedpost every day.
A t its bed it snuggles up.
T iger-like pussycat, fiercer every day.

Mathilda Ward (8)
Wilmcote CE Primary School, Wilmcote

Flower

Flower, flower in the sky
Come down and say goodbye
Don't, don't, don't cry
Because you are beautiful like a butterfly
Bright and colourful in the sky
That's how you are
Now will you say goodbye?

Jennifer Bishop
Wilmcote CE Primary School, Wilmcote

Fairies

F airy wings are delicate,
A ll have fairy wands,
I love fairies with their silk dresses,
R iding bees and birds,
I 've never ever seen a fairy in my life,
E verywhere I look I can never find a fairy.
S trawberries are their favourite food.

Joanna Brookes (8)
Wilmcote CE Primary School, Wilmcote

Vanilla Ice Cream

V ery yummy, in your tummy,
A nd be careful it's cold, it can be sold.
N ever let it melt, it can drip on your belt.
I f you love it, why not buy it?
L ike it, it's a delight
L et it melt in your mouth, love it in the south.
A lways an appetizer.

Isobel Kynoch (8)
Wilmcote CE Primary School, Wilmcote

Summer

S un is shining then I stop,
U pon a hill I pop.
M ole runs into a hole,
M ouse in the house,
E veryone loves summer,
R emember summer is here.

Charlotte Brain (8)
Wilmcote CE Primary School, Wilmcote

FEATURED AUTHOR:

MADDIE STEWART

Maddie is a children's writer, poet and author who currently lives in Coney Island, Northern Ireland.

Maddie has 5 published children's books, 'Cinders', 'Hal's Sleepover', 'Bertie Rooster', 'Peg' and 'Clever Daddy'. Maddie uses her own unpublished work to provide entertaining, interactive poems and rhyming stories for use in her workshops with children when she visits schools, libraries, arts centres and book festivals.

Favourites are 'Silly Billy, Auntie Millie' and 'I'm a Cool, Cool Kid'. Maddie works throughout Ireland from her home in County Down. She is also happy to work from a variety of bases in England. She has friends and family, with whom she regularly stays, in Leicester, Bedford, London and Ashford (Kent). Maddie's workshops are aimed at 5-11-year-olds. Check out Maddie's website for all her latest news and free poetry resources **www.maddiestewart.com**.

Read on to pick up some fab writing tips!

Nonsense Workshop

IF YOU FIND SILLINESS FUN,
YOU WILL LOVE NONSENSE POEMS.
NONSENSE POEMS MIGHT DESCRIBE SILLY THINGS,
OR PEOPLE, OR SITUATIONS,
OR, ANY COMBINATION OF THE THREE.

For example:

When I got out of bed today,
both my arms had run away.
I sent my feet to fetch them back.
When they came back, toe in hand
I realised what they had planned.
They'd made the breakfast I love most,
buttered spider's eggs on toast.

**One way to find out if you enjoy nonsense poems
is to start with familiar nursery rhymes.
Ask your teacher to read them out,
putting in the names of some children in your class.**

Like this: Troy and Jill went up the hill
to fetch a pail of water.
Troy fell down
and broke his crown
and Jill came tumbling after.

If anyone is upset at the idea of using their name, then don't use it.

Did you find this fun?

Now try changing a nursery rhyme.
Keep the rhythm and the rhyme style, but invent a silly situation.

Like this: Hickory Dickory Dare
a pig flew up in the air.
The clouds above
gave him a shove
Hickory Dickory Dare.

Or this: Little Miss Mabel
sat at her table
eating a strawberry pie
but a big, hairy beast
stole her strawberry feast
and made poor little Mabel cry.

How does your rhyme sound if you put your own name in it?

Another idea for nonsense poems is to pretend letters are people
and have them do silly things.

For example:

Mrs A	Mrs B	Mrs C
Lost her way	Dropped a pea	Ate a tree

To make your own 'Silly People Poem', think of a word to use.
To show you an example, I will choose the word 'silly'.
Write your word vertically down the left hand side of your page.
Then write down some words which rhyme
with the sound of each letter.

S mess, dress, Bess, chess, cress
I eye, bye, sky, guy, pie, sky
L sell, bell, shell, tell, swell, well
L " " " " " " (" means the same as written above)
Y (the same words as those rhyming with I)

Use your rhyming word lists to help you make up your poem.

Mrs S made a mess
Mrs I ate a pie
Mrs L rang a bell
Mrs L broke a shell
Mrs Y said 'Bye-bye.'

You might even make a 'Silly Alphabet' by using
all the letters of the alphabet.

It is hard to find rhyming words for all the letters.
H, X and W are letters which are hard to match with rhyming words.
I'll give you some I've thought of:

H - cage, stage, wage (close but not perfect)
X - flex, specs, complex, Middlesex
W - trouble you, chicken coop, bubble zoo

However, with nonsense poems, you can use nonsense words.
You can make up your own words.

To start making up nonsense words you could
try mixing dictionary words together.
Let's make up some nonsense animals.

Make two lists of animals. (You can include birds and fish as well.)

Your lists can be as long as you like. These are lists I made:

elephant	kangaroo
tiger	penguin
lizard	octopus
monkey	chicken

Now use the start of an animal on one list and substitute
it for the start of an animal from your other list.

I might use the start of oct/opus ... oct and substitute it for the end of l/izard
to give me a new nonsense animal ... an octizard.
I might swap the start of monk/ey ... monk with the end of kang/aroo
To give me another new nonsense animal ... a monkaroo.

What might a monkaroo look like? What might it eat?

You could try mixing some food words in the same way,
to make up nonsense foods.

cabbage	potatoes
lettuce	parsley
bacon	crisps

Cribbage, bacley, and lettatoes are some nonsense foods
made up from my lists.

Let's see if I can make a nonsense poem about my monkaroo.

My monkaroo loves bacley.
He'll eat lettatoes too
But his favourite food is cribbage
Especially if it's blue.

Would you like to try and make up your own nonsense poem?

**Nonsense words don't have to be a combination of dictionary words.
They can be completely 'made up'.
You can use nonsense words to write nonsense sonnets,
or list poems or any type of poem you like.**

Here is a poem full of nonsense words:

I melly micked a turdle
and flecked a pendril's tum.
I plotineyed a shugat
and dracked a pipin's plum.

**Ask your teacher to read it putting in some children's names instead
of the first I, and he or she instead of the second I.**

Did that sound funny?

You might think that nonsense poems are just silly and not for the serious poet.
However poets tend to love language. Making up your own words is a natural
part of enjoying words and sounds and how they fit together. Many poets love the
freedom nonsense poems give them. Lots and lots of very famous poets have written
nonsense poems. I'll name some: **Edward Lear**, **Roger McGough**, **Lewis Carroll**,
Jack Prelutsky and **Nick Toczek**. Can you or your teacher think of any more?
For help with a class nonsense poem or to find more nonsense nursery rhymes look
on my website, **www.maddiestewart.com**. Have fun! Maddie Stewart.

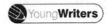

POETRY TECHNIQUES

HERE IS a SELECTION OF POETRY TECHNIQUES WITH EXAMPLES

Metaphors & Similes

A *metaphor* is when you describe your subject *as* something else, for example:
'Winter is a cruel master leaving the servants in a bleak wilderness'
whereas a *simile* describes your subject *like* something else i.e.
'His blue eyes are like ice-cold puddles' or 'The flames flickered like eyelashes'.

Personification

This is to simply give a personality to something that is not human, for example
'Fear spreads her uneasiness around' or 'Summer casts down her warm sunrays'.

Imagery

To use words to create mental pictures of what you are trying to convey,
your poem should awaken the senses and make the reader
feel like they are in that poetic scene …
'The sky was streaked with pink and red as shadows
cast across the once-golden sand'.
'The sea gently lapped the shore as the palm trees rustled softly
in the evening breeze'.

Assonance & Alliteration

Alliteration uses a repeated constant sound and this effect can be quite striking:
'Smash, slippery snake slithered sideways'.
Assonance repeats a significant vowel or vowel sound to create an impact:
'The pool looked cool'.

Poetry Techniques

Repetition

By repeating a significant word the echo effect can be a very powerful way
of enhancing an emotion or point your poem is putting across.
'The blows rained down, down,
Never ceasing,
Never caring
About the pain,
The pain'.

Onomatopoeia

This simply means you use words that sound like the noise you
are describing, for example 'The rain *pattered* on the window'
or 'The tin can *clattered* up the alley'.

Rhythm & Metre

The *rhythm* of a poem means 'the beat', the sense of movement you create.
The placing of punctuation and the use of syllables affect the *rhythm* of the poem.
If your intention is to have your poem read slowly, use double, triple or larger
syllables and punctuate more often, where as if you want to have a fast-paced read
use single syllables, less punctuation and shorter sentences.
If you have a regular rhythm throughout your poem this is known as *metre*.

Enjambment

This means you don't use punctuation at the end of your line, you simply let the line
flow on to the next one. It is commonly used and is a good word to drop into your
homework!

Tone & Lyric

The poet's intention is expressed through their *tone*. You may feel happiness, anger,
confusion, loathing or admiration for your poetic subject. Are you criticising
or praising? How you feel about your topic will affect your choice of words and
therefore your *tone*. For example 'I *loved* her', 'I *cared* for her', 'I *liked* her'.
If you write the poem from a personal view or experience this is referred
to as a *lyrical* poem. A good example of a lyrical poem is Seamus Heaney's
'Mid-term Break' or any sonnet!

All About Shakespeare

Try this fun quiz with your family, friends or even in class!

1. Where was Shakespeare born?

....

2. Mercutio is a character in which Shakepeare play?

....

3. Which monarch was said to be 'quite a fan' of his work?

....

4. How old was he when he married?

....

5. What is the name of the last and 'only original' play he wrote?

....

6. What are the names of King Lear's three daughters?

....

7. Who is Anne Hathaway?

....

8. Which city is the play 'Othello' set in?

....

9. Can you name 2 of Shakespeare's 17 comedies?

....

10. 'This day is call'd the feast of Crispian: He that outlives this day, and comes safe home, Will stand a tip-toe when this day is nam'd, and rouse him at the name of Crispian' is a quote from which play?

....

11. Leonardo DiCaprio played Romeo in the modern day film version of Romeo and Juliet. Who played Juliet in the movie?

....

12. Three witches famously appear in which play?

....

13. Which famous Shakespearean character is Eric in the image to the left?

....

14. What was Shakespeare's favourite poetic form?

....

Answers are printed on the last page of the book, good luck!

If you would rather try the quiz online, you can do so at www.youngwriters.co.uk.

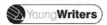

POETRY ACTIVITY

WORD SOUP

To help you write a poem, or even a story, on any theme, you should create word soup!

If you have a theme or subject for your poem, base your word soup on it. If not, don't worry, the word soup will help you find a theme.

To start your word soup you need ingredients:

- Nouns (names of people, places, objects, feelings, i.e. Mum, Paris, house, anger)
- Colours
- Verbs ('doing words', i.e. kicking, laughing, running, falling, smiling)
- Adjectives (words that describe nouns, i.e. tall, hairy, hollow, smelly, angelic)

We suggest at least 5 of each from the above list, this will make sure your word soup has plenty of choice. Now, if you have already been given a theme or title for your poem, base your ingredients on this. If you have no idea what to write about, write down whatever you like, or ask a teacher or family member to give you a theme to write about.

Poetry Activity

Making Word Soup

Next, you'll need a sheet of paper.
Cut it into at least 20 pieces. Make sure the pieces are big enough to write your ingredients on, one ingredient on each piece of paper.
Write your ingredients on the pieces of paper.
Shuffle the pieces of paper and put them all in a box or bowl
- something you can pick the paper out of without looking at the words.
Pick out 5 words to start and use them to write your poem!

Example:

Our theme is winter. Our ingredients are:
- Nouns: snowflake, Santa, hat, Christmas, snowman.
- Colours: blue, white, green, orange, red.
- Verbs: ice-skating, playing, laughing, smiling, wrapping.
- Adjectives: cold, tall, fast, crunchy, sparkly.

Our word soup gave us these 5 words:
snowman, red, cold, hat, fast and our poem goes like this:

It's a *cold* winter's day,
My nose and cheeks are *red*
As I'm outside, building my *snowman*,
I add a *hat* and a carrot nose to finish,
I hope he doesn't melt too *fast*!

Tip: add more ingredients to your word soup
and see how many different poems you can write!

Tip: if you're finding it hard to write a poem with
the words you've picked, swap a word with another one!

Tip: try adding poem styles and techniques,
such as assonance or haiku to your soup for an added challenge!

YOUNG WRITERS INFORMATION

We hope you have enjoyed reading this book - and that you will continue to enjoy it in the coming years.

If you like reading and writing poetry drop us a line, or give us a call, and we'll send you a free information pack.

Alternatively, if you would like to order further copies of this book or any of our other titles, then please give us a call or log onto our website at www.youngwriters.co.uk.

Young Writers Information
Remus House
Coltsfoot Drive
Peterborough
PE2 9BF
Tel: (01733) 890066
Fax: (01733) 313524

Email: info@youngwriters.co.uk

SHAKESPEARE QUIZ ANSWERS

1. Stratford-upon-Avon **2.** Romeo and Juliet **3.** James I **4.** 18 **5.** The Tempest **6.** Regan, Cordelia and Goneril **7.** His wife **8.** Venice **9.** All's Well That Ends Well, As You Like It, The Comedy of Errors, Cymbeline, Love's Labour's Lost, Measure for Measure, The Merchant of Venice, The Merry Wives of Windsor, A Midsummer Night's Dream, Much Ado About Nothing, Pericles - Prince of Tyre, The Taming of the Shrew, The Tempest, Twelfth Night, The Two Gentlemen of Verona, Troilus & Cressida, The Winter's Tale **10.** Henry V **11.** Claire Danes **12.** Macbeth **13.** Hamlet **14.** Sonnet